# THE IMPORTANCE OF

# Dr. Seuss

*These and other titles are included in The Importance Of biography series:*

# THE IMPORTANCE OF

# Dr. Seuss

### by Stuart P. Levine

Lucent Books, P.O. Box 289011, San Diego, CA 92198-9011

*To Wendy,*
*for keeping the wonder alive.*

Library of Congress Cataloging-in-Publication Data

Levine, Stuart P., 1968–
    Dr. Seuss / by Stuart P. Levine.
        p.   cm.—(The importance of)
    Includes bibliographical references and index.
    Summary: Profiles the life and work of author Dr. Seuss,
including his childhood, life as a struggling cartoonist, his
career, the use of politics, morals, and animation in his
books, and his lasting legacy.
    ISBN 1-56006-748-9  (alk. paper)
    1. Seuss, Dr.—Juvenile literature. 2. Authors, American—
20th century—Biography—Juvenile literature. 3. Illustrators
—United States—Biography—Juvenile literature. 4. Children's
literature—Authorship—Juvenile literature. [1. Seuss, Dr.
2. Authors, American. 3. Illustrators.] I. Title. II. Series.
    PS3513.E2 Z73   2001
    813'.52—dc21                                         00–009242

# Contents

# Foreword

THE IMPORTANCE OF biography series deals with individuals who have made a unique contribution to history. The editors of the series have deliberately chosen to cast a wide net and include people from all fields of endeavor. Individuals from politics, music, art, literature, philosophy, science, sports, and religion are all represented. In addition, the editors did not restrict the series to individuals whose accomplishments have helped change the course of history. Of necessity, this criterion would have eliminated many whose contribution was great, though limited. Charles Darwin, for example, was responsible for radically altering the scientific view of the natural history of the world. His achievements continue to impact the study of science today. Others, such as Chief Joseph of the Nez Percé, played a pivotal role in the history of their own people. While Joseph's influence does not extend much beyond the Nez Percé, his nonviolent resistance to white expansion and his continuing role in protecting his tribe and his homeland remain an inspiration to all.

These biographies are more than factual chronicles. Each volume attempts to emphasize an individual's contributions both in his or her own time and for posterity. For example, the voyages of Christopher Columbus opened the way to European colonization of the New World. Unquestionably, his encounter with the New World brought monumental changes to both Europe and the Americas in his day. Today, however, the broader impact of Columbus's voyages is being critically scrutinized. *Christopher Columbus,* as well as every biography in The Importance Of series, includes and evaluates the most recent scholarship available on each subject.

Each author includes a wide variety of primary and secondary source quotations to document and substantiate his or her work. All quotes are footnoted to show readers exactly how and where biographers derive their information, as well as provide stepping stones to further research. These quotations enliven the text by giving readers eyewitness views of the life and times of each individual covered in The Importance Of series.

Finally, each volume is enhanced by photographs, bibliographies, chronologies, and comprehensive indexes. For both the casual reader and the student engaged in research, The Importance Of biographies will be a fascinating adventure into the lives of people who have helped shape humanity's past and present, and who will continue to shape its future.

# IMPORTANT DATES IN THE LIFE OF DR. SEUSS

**1943–1946**
Serves in the U.S. Army Signal Corps, Information and Education Division, and works on films such as *Your Job in Germany*, which earned an Academy Award under the title *Hitler Lives?*

**1927**
Sells first cartoon to the *Saturday Evening Post* and marries Helen Palmer on November 29.

**1904**
Theodor Seuss Geisel is born in Springfield, Massachusetts, on March 2.

**1940**
*Horton Hatches the Egg* is published.

**1937**
Publishes *And to Think That I Saw It on Mulberry Street* with Vanguard Press, launching his children's book career.

**1952**
*The 5,000 Fingers of Dr. T* is released.

**1950**
*If I Ran the Zoo* is published and named a Caldecott Honor Book.

*If I Ran the Circus* is publish[ed] receives his first honorary d[oc]torate from Dartmou[th]

| 1900 | 1920 | 1925 | 1930 | 1935 | 1940 | 1945 | 1950 | 19 |

**1921–1925**
Attends Dartmouth College, where he writes for the humor magazine the *Jack-O'-Lantern* and earns his bachelor's degree.

**1928**
Begins "Quick Henry, the Flit" ad campaign.

**1939**
Moves to Random House and publishes *The Seven Lady Godivas* and *The King's Stilts*.

**1941–1942**
Works as an editorial political cartoonist for *PM*, a liberal newspaper.

**1947**
*McElligot's Pool* is published and chosen as a Caldecott Honor Book; wins another Academy Award for *Design for Death* (another remake of one of his army films).

**1951**
Wins third Academy Award for *Gerald McBoing-Boing*.

**1954**
*Horton Hears a Who!* is published.

**1958**
*The Cat in the Hat Comes Back* and *Yertle the Turtle and Other Stories* are published.

**1977**
Receives an Emmy award for *Halloween Is Grinch Night* and another honorary doctorate from Lake Forest College.

**1998**
The first annual Read Across America Day in honor of Dr. Seuss's birthday occurs on March 2.

**1991**
*Six by Seuss: A Treasury of Dr. Seuss Classics* is published; Theodor Seuss Geisel dies on September 24 at the age of eighty-seven.

**1961**
*The Sneetches and Other Stories* is published; *Ten Apples Up on Top!* is published under the name Theo. LeSieg.

**1968**
*The Eye Book* (Theo. LeSieg) and *The Foot Book*, the first of the Bright and Early Books, are published; marries Audrey Stone Dimond on August 5.

**1985**
Receives another honorary doctorate from Princeton University.

| 1960 | 1965 | 1970 | 1975 | 1980 | 1985 | 1990 | 1995 | 2000 |
|------|------|------|------|------|------|------|------|------|

**1960**
*Green Eggs and Ham* and *One Fish Two Fish Red Fish Blue Fish* are published.

**1971**
*The Lorax* is published; receives a Peabody Award for his television specials *How the Grinch Stole Christmas!* and *Horton Hears a Who!*

**1990**
*Oh, the Places You'll Go!* is published.

**1967**
Helen Palmer Geisel dies on October 23; *The Cat in the Hat Song Book* is published.

**1996**
*A Hatful of Seuss*, another collection of classic Dr. Seuss books, is published.

**1984**
*The Butter Battle Book* is published, causing a stir of great controversy; receives a Pulitzer prize for his contribution to children's literature.

**2000**
Universal Pictures presents the big-budget movie version of *How the Grinch Stole Christmas!* starring Jim Carrey as the Grinch; *The Seussical* opens on Broadway.

**1957**
Two of Dr. Seuss's biggest successes are published, *How the Grinch Stole Christmas!* and *The Cat in the Hat*; the Beginner Books division of Random House is launched.

# "An Imagination with a Long Tail"

For most people, the thought of growing up in a world without Green Eggs and Ham, Grinches, and Cats in Hats is barely conceivable. These odd creations occupy a special place in the earliest memories of children around the world. Having sold more than 200 million copies of his forty-seven books, Dr. Seuss is by far the best-selling children's author to date, and perhaps the most beloved.

Although few children ever knew his real name, the man behind the magic was Theodor Seuss Geisel. For more than fifty years, he wrote books that delighted adults and children. His words and pictures, which range from simply humorous to powerfully insightful, seem to know no age limits. One six-year-old captured this notion while writing a review of a Dr. Seuss book for his school paper; "All ages would like it from 6 to 44—that's how old my mother is."[1]

## A RICH LIFE

Geisel lived a long and adventurous life. Having spent eighty-seven years traveling the globe and experiencing everything he could through the eyes of a child, he was more than qualified to give the world a nonstop parade of fun and fantasy. Born in a small American town, he spent his childhood sketching animals at the local zoo, run by his father, and reading everything he could get his hands on. After graduating from college, he went to England in pursuit of his Ph.D. in English literature. He had always wanted to be an educator, but found the rigors and rules of graduate school too confining.

Upon his return to America, he found success in the advertising industry. It was during this period that he adopted the name Dr. Seuss. Although he never got past the first year of graduate school, the "Dr." became official many years later when he received no fewer than eight honorary doctorate degrees from major universities around the country. Making money and a name for himself with his off-beat ad campaigns wasn't enough though. He still felt unfulfilled and decided to pursue writing children's books. After more than twenty-five rejections of his first book, *And to Think That I Saw It on Mulberry Street*, he found a publisher and learned the valuable lesson of perseverance.

## A CAREER WITHOUT LIMITS

Unlike anything that had been seen in children's literature before, *Mulberry Street* was an instant success and launched his prolific career. For the rest of his life, Dr. Seuss would continue to produce one masterpiece after another. Books like *Horton Hears a Who!*, *If I Ran the Zoo*, *The 500 Hats of Bartholomew Cubbins*, and *Yertle the Turtle* were all early successes. However, *The Cat in the Hat*, the book that would forever cement his place on the map of children's literature, didn't come until he was fifty-three years old. With its publication, Dr. Seuss was launched into the public spotlight—something he had never been comfortable with. *The Cat in the Hat* flew off the shelves at an unprecedented rate, and his adoring fans cried out for more. He did not disappoint them. Later that same year, he released *How the Grinch Stole Christmas!* which would go on to become one of the staples of American holiday television.

Dr. Seuss's works possess several unique qualities, which help them to stand out from other children's books. Chief among these are two important points. First, he always had a profound respect for children. He never spoke down to them or patronized them. Geisel was fond of saying that children have as much right to quality as adults do, and he labored endlessly over every word and illustration to make sure that each book he produced was perfect from start to finish. The second ingredient to his success is far simpler, but perhaps much harder to achieve. His books are always fun. Dr. Seuss challenges people, young and old, to see the hilarity and the insanity that is all around them—and to have a good laugh at it. He accomplished this with a sense of humor and an inexhaustible imagination that some have described as true genius. As one young boy wrote in a fan letter, "Dr. Seuss, you have an imagination with a long tail."[2]

### THE DOCTOR EARNS HIS DOCTORATE

*Dr. Seuss received a total of eight honorary doctorate degrees throughout his life, each one commending him for his contributions to the advancement of children's literature. In 1985, he received one such degree from Princeton University, and the citation, reprinted in* Dr. Seuss from Then to Now, *read as follows:*

"He makes house calls in the land of our first dreams and fears, where naughty cats wear hats, and the menace of the Grinch is real. From Mulberry Street to Solla Sollew he leads us through the brightly colored landscapes of imagination, a place of improbable rhymes and impossible names, odd creatures and curious food. Encouraging children to read beyond zebra, to count fishes red and blue, he gives them their first mastery over the mystery of signs. He shows them the way to the adult world, as he shows adults the way to the child."

*Dr. Seuss, seated with a group of school children in La Jolla, California, 1957, had a profound respect for children and believed they should enjoy reading.*

## MORE THAN MEETS THE EYE

Dr. Seuss did far more than just make the world laugh, however. His dreams of being an educator were realized after the publication of *The Cat in the Hat.* Originally written as an attempt to replace the bland "Dick and Jane"–style reading primers, the book helped him launch a new way of learning. No longer would children be subjected to the boring task of being forced to read. Dr. Seuss pioneered the concept of wrapping quality educational material in fun and engaging stories. His "Beginner Books" would become the standard tools used by teachers and parents to introduce the concept of reading. By making it fun, reading was no longer a chore but an entertaining activity. His books were so much fun, in fact, that children weren't the only ones laughing. Adults no longer found it a chore to read to their children.

Having always had strong views on politics, the environment, and the importance of good moral fiber, some of Geisel's books also reflected messages that he felt strongly about. In the later years of his life, these messages would become clear. He would take on topics such as conservation, nuclear war, and even the meaning of life. By the time he died, in 1991, he had achieved the status of a pop culture hero, spawning college fan clubs and websites. No longer simply a well-known children's author, Dr. Seuss has become a part of American culture. Leaving behind a legacy that continues to enchant a new generation of children, the potent gift of fun, laughter, and learning that he gave to the world will not soon be forgotten. Helen Renthal, a journalist for the *Chicago Tribune,* may have summed it up best when she said, "Somehow, the human race produces what it needs, space ships, or wonder drugs or a Dr. Seuss."[3]

# 1 Dr. Seuss's First Childhood

On March 2, 1904, the quiet town of Springfield, Massachusetts, welcomed the birth of its most famous resident. The child's name was Theodor Seuss Geisel, but he would later become known to the world as Dr. Seuss. Ted, as his family called him, was born to Theodor Robert Geisel and Henrietta (Seuss) Geisel in a small house just around the corner from his grandfather's brewery. He would spend the rest of his childhood growing, learning, and playing in Springfield, and the experiences he had in this nurturing environment, amid wild animals and expert marksmen, would plant the seeds of the man who would become Dr. Seuss.

## "WHO THUNK YOU UP?"

An eight-year-old fan once wrote, "Dear Dr. Seuss, you sure thunk up a lot of funny books. You sure thunk up a million funny animals. . . . Who thunk you up, Dr. Seuss?"[4] Theodor Geisel had a rich life, full of many influences, but his strongest influence may have been his family. Ted had two sisters. His older sister, Marnie, was a playmate and lifelong friend. His younger sister, Henrietta, died of pneumonia when she was less than two years old.

*Theodor Seuss Giesel (shown here as an adult) was raised in a nurturing family which fostered his creativity.*

Ted's mother, also named Henrietta, was an extremely nurturing person. One of his earliest memories was of a stuffed dog she gave him as a small child. Naming

## DOODLING WYNNMPHS

*An article by Robert Sullivan in the December 1995 issue of* Yankee Magazine *discusses the important role that Ted's mother, Henrietta, played in his life. Her unquestioning support would help to foster his creative spirit.*

"Ted was devoted to his mother, and she responded with unceasing praise and encouragement. When Ted decided that riflery wasn't for him, that was fine with Henrietta. When Ted complained that he hated exercising at the school gym, Henrietta defended him to his father. When Ted drew animals on the attic walls with the crayons and pencils he kept by his bedside, that was fine too. When Ted showed his mother a sketch of a beast from the zoo— a beast with ears hanging down to its feet and beyond— Henrietta said that was wonderful. When Ted announced that the animal was called 'a Wynnmph,' she said, of course it is!"

his beloved dog Theophrastus, he kept it with him all his life, ultimately giving it to his stepdaughter on the evening of his death, more than eighty years later.

Ted's mother indulged all his childhood passions and encouraged him in all his artistic and outlandish pursuits. Henrietta took her son to church every Sunday, and she quickly realized that he responded to rhyme and repetition. He knew the words to every hymn and even recited the Old Testament in rhyme:

The great Jehovah speaks to us
In Genesis and Exodus;
Leviticus and numbers, three,
Followed by Deuteronomy.[5]

Ted would later admit that he added the word *three* just to make it rhyme—surely an early sign of his lifelong relationship with wordplay.

Whether in church or at home, Ted's mother always gave him free rein. She didn't even seem to mind when he would use the pencils and crayons he kept by his bed to draw on the walls. Geisel recalls that she helped to foster his creativity early in life by sending the unequivocal message that "Everything you do is great, just go ahead and do it."[6]

## FATHER KNOWS BEST

Theodor Sr. also influenced his son's outlook on life. He was a driven man who worked very hard and instilled in his son the importance of discipline. Theodor Sr. was an expert marksman and, according to Ted, he would "practice target shooting for a half hour every morning in hopes of breaking the world target shooting record.

He taught me the importance of seeking perfection."[7] In fact, his father had already earned the world's record once, in 1902, for shooting at two hundred yards. Later in life, Ted would keep the framed bull's-eye from that competition hanging above his drawing board to remind himself to always strive for perfection.

## THE GERMAN BREWERY

Ted's grandfather was a German immigrant. When he arrived in America, he and a partner opened what became a very successful family business, the Kalmback and Geisel Brewery (which the local townspeople jokingly referred to as the Come Back and Guzzle Brewery). The brewery was a very important part of the town, and as a result the Geisels were a well-known and respected family for the early part of Ted's life.

Ted had fond memories of his family's pride in their heritage. They would often speak German at home and join other members of the town's German American population in a variety of social activities. However, this pride would soon turn to a source of pain for young Ted and his sister.

## WORLD WAR I

On April 6, 1917, the United States entered World War I. Suddenly, Ted's German descent was no longer a mantle of pride but one of shame. The widespread anti-German sentiment that pervaded the country during this time was difficult on him. German books were removed from library shelves, and there were reports of Germans being stoned in nearby cities. Ted and his sister Marnie would discuss ways to avoid harassment at school. Even the Kalmback and Geisel Brewery changed its

*Anti-German sentiment in the United States during World War I left young Theodor Geisel feeling excluded and persecuted.*

name to the Liberty Brewery in an effort to avoid a boycott. This childhood persecution may have been the origin of Ted's lifelong feeling of separation from the rest of the adult world. The books he later became famous for were often written about characters who were different, excluded, or persecuted.

## TEDDY ROOSEVELT

An effort to prove his patriotism resulted in an event that would haunt Ted for the rest of his life. He joined the Boy Scouts and became a very active member. He played the bugle for his local troop, and when they had a fund-raiser selling war bonds, Ted managed to rack up the second highest sales record in the troop. As a whole, his troop was among the top sellers in the country, and former president Teddy Roosevelt came to Springfield to award medals to the top ten scouts.

With his family beaming with pride and the entire town gathered for the ceremony, Ted went up to receive his award. Due to an error, however, Roosevelt hadn't been given enough medals and when Ted, who was last in line, stepped up, the former president just stared at him and asked what he was doing there. Humiliated, Ted was ushered off the stage, and ever since, he dreaded public appearances. This hampered him later in life, for he was often asked to make public addresses in person or on television. He avoided them whenever possible, often canceling at the last moment. When he could not avoid an appearance, he was riddled with fear. On

one occasion, he even suffered a panic attack while appearing on a live television talk show program.

## EARLY INFLUENCES

Despite a few unpleasant occurrences growing up, Ted's childhood was generally filled with many wonderful experiences. He played tenor banjo as well as the mandolin. He acted in school plays and enjoyed working as an usher at the local movie theater. His talent for humor began to surface early, as he wrote jokes for his high school newspaper. He was voted by his classmates "class artist" and "class wit."

The small town of Springfield was full of memorable people and events that would shape significant parts of Ted's life. The names of neighbors like Terwilliger, Wickersham, and McElligot would resurface later as major characters in his books. And the fantastic parades that would careen down Main Street during holidays, for example, would later serve as the influence for his very first children's book, *And to Think That I Saw It on Mulberry Street*.

## TED'S FIRST "BIG BANG"

At the age of twelve, Ted entered the local newspaper's advertising contest and won first place with a cartoon of a man reeling in an enormous fish. He recalled this personal achievement as his first "big bang."[8] Later in life, Ted would make a living, and a name for himself, in the advertising business.

## THE ROAD LESS TRAVELED

*Geisel felt strongly that following the straight and narrow path in life isn't always the best route to success. In the book* Pipers at the Gates of Dawn *by Jonathan Cott, Geisel recounts the story of having learned this lesson through his father's seeming misfortune.*

"You see, my father, among other things, ran a zoo in Springfield, Massachusetts. He was a guy who became president of a Springfield brewery the day Prohibition was declared (this was wartime prohibition). So he became very cynical and sat for days in the living room saying 'S.O.B., S.O.B.' over and over—he didn't know what to do with himself. But he had been honorary head of the Parks Department, and there had been a mix-up with the books and he had to straighten them out. At that time the superintendent left the park system, so my father took the job permanently. And at a salary of five thousand dollars a year he became a philanthropist. He built tennis courts, trout streams, three golf courses, bowling greens—he changed people's lives more than he would have done if he'd been a millionaire; he used WPA funds and government money to put people to work. So he ended up a very worthwhile guy."

Another memorable Springfield influence involved the Forest Park Library and Johnson's Book Store. An avid reader from an early age, Ted spent countless hours reading and loved visiting these two places. He regularly stopped by the library on his way home from school, and when he brought home good grades, his mother rewarded him with a trip to the book store, where he could buy one book of his choice. One of his favorite childhood books was *The Hole Book*, and he read it over and over. The book was about a bullet that ricochets and rebounds through a house, putting holes in everything. Each page of the book had a hole through it, showing where the bullet had

been. The bullet makes its way through everything, including a water boiler, which causes the house to flood, and is eventually stopped by an extremely hard cake. Clearly, Ted had a love of the surreal and whimsical from a very young age.

## A POWERFUL LESSON FROM DAD

A common theme that seems to have run through Ted's life was creating success out of adversity. As a teenager, he watched his father learn this very lesson. Theodor Sr. had spent his disciplined life working hard at his father's brewery, allowing his personal interests, such as inventing and

*Main Street in Springfield, Massachusetts was the influence for Dr. Seuss's first book* And to Think That I Saw It on Mulberry Street.

volunteering for the local parks department, to always take a back seat. All these years of diligent toil were meant to pay off when grandfather Geisel retired and Theodor Sr. took over as president of the company. The very day this was supposed to happen, a law called Prohibition was enacted by the U.S. government, making the sale of alcohol illegal. Thus, despite his years of hard work, Theodor Sr. was out of a job. Ted later recalled that this event changed his father significantly. Theodor Sr. became sullen and cynical. He sat around the house for days at a time yelling and cursing. After thirty-five years of working toward a very specific goal, he was completely lost.

Ted's father began to spend more time at the volunteer job he loved, working with the Springfield Parks Commission. Eventually, he was given the paid position of parks superintendent, where he re-

mained for the rest of his working days. He used his position, and some of his own money, to build tennis courts, golf courses, trout streams, and a variety of other recreational outlets for the town. He also provided the townspeople with jobs, building all these improvements over many years.

Later in life, Ted realized the profound influence this turn of events had on him. The lesson he learned was that the straight and narrow pursuit of a goal was no guarantee for success. Sometimes greater riches could be found by taking a less conventional path. His father's years of hard work at something he saw as a family obligation did not pay off. Yet by doing something he loved, he was able to change the face of an entire town. This became a persistent theme not only in Ted's life but also in many of his books: Life's bumpier roads are often the ones worth taking.

## THE ZOO

Theodor Sr.'s strongest passion within the parks system was the local zoo. He had been active in its operation and expansion for many years before he took over the Parks Commission. The Geisels' home on Fairfield Street was near enough to the zoo that Ted would sit up at night, listening to the symphony created by the roars and songs of the animals. He loved the zoo and spent a lot of time there with his father. Being permitted in the back areas gave young Ted personal encounters with many of the creatures that lived there. He was fascinated with the incredible diversity of the animal kingdom and spent countless hours observing, learning about, and sketching the animals. He often created surreal versions of the animals in his sketches, adding wings to a tiger or long floppy ears to a giraffe. The time he spent at the zoo had a powerful impact on him, as can be seen in the endless parade of animal creatures he later created, from Sneetches and the Lorax to the Grinch and the Cat in the Hat.

This love of animals followed him into adulthood and was the inspiration for many of his globe-hopping vacations. He loved to travel to exotic places and see new animal species. Although the world later embraced his unusual creations, Ted's early drawings met with some criticism. When Ted was in high school, he enrolled in an art class. On the first day, the

### SCHOOL'S NOT FOR EVERYONE

*In Jonathan Cott's* Pipers at the Gates of Dawn, *Ted talks about his unique drawing style and a discouraging art teacher who may have unwittingly helped shape it.*

"My style of drawing animals derives from the fact that I don't know how to draw. I began drawing pictures as a child . . . trying, let's say, to get as close to a lion as possible; people would laugh, so I decided to go for the laugh. I can't draw normally. I think I could draw normally if I wanted to, but I see no reason to re-create something that's already created. If I'd gone to art school I'd never have been successful. In fact, I did attend one art class in high school. And at one point during the class I turned the painting I was working on upside down—I didn't exactly know what I was doing, but actually I was checking the balance: If something is wrong with the composition upside down, then something's wrong with it the other way. And the teacher said, 'Theodor, real artists don't turn their paintings upside down.' It's the only reason I went on [in the field]—to prove that teacher wrong."

class was working on a drawing and Ted's teacher, taking one look at his work, told him that he would never learn to draw. The teacher wanted him to draw in a more realistic manner. "That teacher wanted me to draw the world as it is," Geisel recalled in an interview many years later. "I wanted to draw things as I saw them."[9] That day, he dropped the class and never went back.

He attributes much of the success of his odd creations to this event. His lack of formal art training kept him from being pushed in one direction or another and allowed him to create a style that was truly unique. "I've capitalized on my mistakes," he said. "Since I can't draw, I've taken the awkwardness and peculiarities of my natural style and developed them."[10]

## THE SCHOOL PAPER

Some of Ted's other high school teachers were more supportive. One had a particular influence on him. Red Smith, an English teacher, was very encouraging to his students, never condemning what they wrote but offering suggestions on how to make it better. Under Smith's guidance, Ted became very active in the school's paper, drawing cartoons and writing jokes called "grinds." He also wrote a number of articles and commentaries under pseudonyms, or pen names, such as Pete the Pessimist and T. S. LeSieg (a name he would write under again later in life). Eventually, Ted became the humor editor for the paper. Several of Ted's friends were just as enthralled with Red Smith as he was, and

when it came time to go to college, Ted and a dozen of his classmates chose their favorite teacher's alma mater, Dartmouth.

## LIFE IN COLLEGE

In September 1921, Ted enrolled in college and chose to major in English. He was also interested in pledging a fraternity during his freshman year, but he did not receive a single invitation. A little dejected, he found himself with a lot of free time on his hands and again became involved in a number of school publications. He worked on the school newspaper, but his real interest lay in Dartmouth's humor magazine, the *Jack-O'-Lantern*. *Jacko*, as it was called, became his home away from home. He became good friends with the magazine's editor, an upperclassman, and they spent many late nights working on cartoons and jokes. Ted was determined to be the *Jacko* editor someday.

At Dartmouth, he was again graced with a number of good friends and influences. One of his professors, William K. Stewart, always padded his lectures with stories of his travel and adventures in Europe. These stories were fascinating to Ted, and served as a strong motivation for him to pursue travels of his own. Later in life, Ted would spend several weeks out of every year traveling abroad and learning about other countries and cultures. He drew on these extensive travels as both a resource and an inspiration for the books he wrote.

As in high school, an English teacher, this one a creative writing professor, be-

*Dr. Seuss attended Dartmouth College (pictured), and his cartoons became a staple in the school's humor magazine, the* Jack-O'-Lantern.

came an important figure during Ted's college years. This professor was extremely encouraging and would have students over to his house, where they would eat, drink cocoa, create, and read their stories. Ted loved these evenings and boasted that he could write something creative on virtually any subject. He proved it by writing a humorous "book review" of the Boston and Maine Railroad timetables.

One of Ted's close friends at Dartmouth, Pete Blodgett, may have unwittingly been the inspiration for one of Dr. Seuss's most famous characters. Blodgett had a beagle he took with him everywhere, including class. The beagle caught the attention of one professor and got the two friends invited on a hunting trip. Dur-ing the excursion, Ted sketched a number of things, including Blodgett's beagle with antlers. This drawing may have been a precursor to the Grinch's pitiful dog, forced to wear antlers and haul an enormous load of stolen Christmas loot.

## A First Taste of Success

Ted's cartoons quickly became a staple of the *Jack-O'-Lantern*, and he gained recognition throughout campus for his work. By his sophomore year, the fraternities were knocking on his door, and he pledged Sigma Phi Epsilon. He also became a member of a number of other social and academic societies. Amid all this, he found time to become the manager of the soccer team and play mandolin in the orchestra.

His true love at Dartmouth, however, remained the *Jacko*, and by the end of his junior year, he fulfilled his ambition to become the magazine's editor in chief.

Up until this point, Ted had struggled between his twin interests of drawing and writing. It was through his work at *Jacko* that Ted claims to have first realized the potential of blending words with pictures.

> "I began to get it through my skull that words and pictures were Yin and Yang. . . . I began thinking that words and pictures, married, might possibly produce a progeny more interesting than either parent. It took me almost a

quarter of a century to find the proper way [to do this]. At Dartmouth I couldn't even get them engaged."[11]

## THE BIRTH OF SEUSS

Ted was known among his friends to be a bit of a clown and even a practical joker. Ironically, he was voted by one of his social clubs as "Least Likely to Succeed," because he never took anything seriously. Toward the end of his senior year at Dartmouth, Ted and some friends were caught in the act of having a little too much fun. Prohibition, a federal law that made it illegal to possess alcohol, was still in effect,

---

### FROM MAN TO STATUE

*The small Massachusetts town that Ted grew up in not only helped shape the person he would become but also served as the inspiration for many of his characters. An article by Herbert Kupferberg in the June 7, 1998,* Palm Beach Post's Parade Magazine *describes a memorial being built by the town in Ted's honor.*

"As all loyal readers of Dr. Seuss know—or should know—the very first of his books, which was published in 1937, was called *And to Think [That] I Saw it on Mulberry Street*. There are dozens of Mulberry Streets in cities and towns across the U.S. But this particular one is to be found in Springfield, Mass., where Dr. Seuss . . . was born in 1904, the son of that city's superintendent of parks. And it was there that he imagined his first dizzying procession of fantastic animals, bizarre vehicles, and bemused children. Now Springfield is planning to build a $4 million memorial to the good doctor, who died in 1991 at the age of 87. It will be the kind of open-air memorial where the Cat in the Hat would be free to romp, Horton would find room to hatch an egg, and even the Grinch might feel happy. For it will be part of a pleasant park area abounding in greenery . . . and friendly statues standing everywhere to remind visitors of the zany, wonderful world that Ted Geisel brought to life in his many books."

*While at college Dr. Seuss (shown here with one of his drawings) struggled to find a perfect blend of words and pictures.*

and the landlord of his apartment turned him and his friends in to the dean for drinking alcohol. Ted failed to see the harm, as there was a single pint of gin in a room of ten people. Nonetheless, they had broken the law, and part of Ted's disciplinary action involved being stripped of his position as the editor of *Jacko*. In addition to losing his title, he would no longer be allowed to write for the magazine.

Unwilling to accept defeat, he refused to let this setback stop him, and once again proved that adversity could lead to success. Ted was determined to continue writing for *Jacko* during his remaining months at college, but he could not afford to use his own name and risk expulsion. Hence, for the first time in his life, he began signing his cartoons, "Seuss" (the "Dr." would come later).

# 2 The Struggling Cartoonist

Ted's love of language helped him to decide what his next step after Dartmouth should be. He wanted to pursue a doctorate of English literature at Oxford University in England. Dartmouth offered an Oxford fellowship to its alumni, so Ted applied for the grant and called his father to tell him of his plans. Beaming with pride, the senior Geisel told a number of friends about Ted's plans. The next day, the cover story of the local Springfield newspaper reported that young Ted Geisel would be going to Oxford on a full scholarship to earn his Ph.D. Ted found out a short time later, however, that he did not receive the fellowship. Refusing to lose face in his community, Theodor Sr. scrounged up enough money to send his son to Oxford.

## GRADUATE SCHOOL

Leaving his friends and family half a world away, Ted headed off to England, in the fall of 1925, to pursue his doctorate. This trip was the beginning of a lifelong obsession with travel.

Ted didn't last very long at Oxford, however. His pranks and disregard for the rules quickly led to his falling out of favor

*Students leaving classes at Oxford University in 1925 where Dr. Seuss enrolled the same year.*

with the school's administrators. On one occasion, unable to accept the rule against lowerclassmen having vehicles on campus, Ted bought a motorcycle and dressed it up with dead ducks so he could drive it on campus, masquerading as a poultry shop delivery boy.

In class he found himself uninterested and unable to concentrate on the material. The margins of his graduate school notebooks were filled with doodles and illustrations. One of those notebooks, which still exists in a private collection, clearly shows how his interest waned over the semester. As the pages progress, the doodles crept out from the margins, usurping more and more space until, toward the end of the semester, there were few class notes and full pages of cartoons.

One day, an American classmate named Helen Palmer happened to see his drawings. She leaned over in class and told him that he was wasting his time in school. She said his cartoons were wonderful and that he should attempt to make a living at that instead. He ended up taking her advice (and, a few years later, her hand in marriage).

Ted's faculty adviser agreed with Helen and suggested that he "take a year off to tour Europe, visit museums, read and improve his knowledge of history."[12] Years later, in an interview for his college alumni paper, Ted recalled that the final straw that caused him to leave Oxford was an excruciating class in Shakespearean punctuation, which he claimed was the dullest thing he had ever had to do. His professor "had dug up all the old Shakespearean folios [manuscripts] and lamented that some

had more semicolons than commas. And some had more commas than periods. . . . I listened for a while," Geisel said, "and then went to my room and packed."[13]

## OFF TO SEE THE WORLD

Never content to stay in one place, Geisel would spend much of his life exploring the farthest reaches of the world. After less than a year at Oxford, Ted decided to leave school and travel. His family came to visit him and together they toured Europe. They spent a lot of time in Germany, visiting relatives and becoming acquainted with their ancestral roots. Their last stop was Paris, and when his family went back to the States, Ted decided to stay.

Without his parents to pay the bills, Geisel was forced to watch what he spent, so as not to deplete the small savings he had with him. Despite his lack of funds, Ted later referred to those days as some of the best in his life. He spent time sitting in parks and on Paris street corners attempting to write a best-selling novel. He even recalled having frequently encountered a young writer named Ernest Hemingway engaged in the very same activity.

## EUROPE AWAITS

After another brief trip to Germany, Geisel returned to Paris and sought out one of his old Oxford professors who had begun teaching at the Sorbonne University. Ted had a lot of respect for this particular man and wanted his advice on where to go with his graduate career.

Geisel had a strong passion for literature and education and didn't want to just give up pursuing it. The professor was an authority on the author Jonathan Swift and, knowing that Ted was fond of Swift, suggested a research project. He explained that although Swift's early writings had turned up a treasure trove of work, there was a gap. No one had come across anything Swift had written between the ages of sixteen and seventeen. He suggested that Ted spend the next few years researching this. If he could find any of the lost material and put it together into a critical thesis, he would probably earn his doctorate. However, if Swift hadn't written anything during that period, all his time would be wasted. To Ted, this sounded like a colossal waste of time. He recalled thanking the professor, walking out of his house, and booking passage on a cattle boat to Corsica, Italy, where he proceeded "to paint donkeys for a month."[14]

It was at this point that the young Dr. Seuss decided that adults take life way too seriously. He vowed to always view the world from a child's perspective: experiencing, reacting to, and enjoying life, rather than studying it. This attitude would carry him through the rest of his life and most likely led to his uncanny ability to engage children with his stories.

Still waiting for Helen to finish school, Ted continued to travel. A love of art history made Italy the perfect place for him

## CARTOON LESSONS

*In her biography* Dr. Seuss, *Ruth K. MacDonald discusses how Ted's early cartooning experience helped lay the groundwork for his later successes.*

"Of all the influences most directly observable on Seuss's illustration, his experience in drawing cartoons in college deserves special mention. The single panel containing both text and picture, and the limited number of panels for each comic strip, forced an economy of language and illustration, which would serve the author well in his writing for children. At the same time, the artwork could be less than great art, as long as it was expressive. In the cartoon strip, artwork needs to carry the message beyond what the language can do. Seuss's understanding of the cartoon strip dynamic is one of the most popularizing of his techniques. To tell a story in miniature, with emphasis on the visual, is perfect preparatory experience for writing an interesting book for the very young, one that will capture and hold their interest, while at the same time encouraging them to read."

*A boy sells copies of the* Saturday Evening Post *in New York City during the 1920s. Dr. Seuss sold his first cartoon to the magazine, prompting him to move to the city and begin a career as a freelance cartoonist.*

at the time. He spent a lot of time painting and drawing. He describes the time as his Roman and Florentine period, as he drew primarily images of the Madonna. Many of his paintings were caricatures, and in one case a passing tourist from the States noted his work titled *The Madonna of the Roller Skates* and commented to Ted that he appeared to be in a stage of adolescent revolt that he might someday overcome, an occurrence Dr. Seuss found unlikely.

Geisel also wrote a book while in Rome, but it would never be the great American novel he had hoped to sell. "It turned out not to be so great, so I boiled it down to the Great American Short Story. It wasn't very great in that form either. Two years later, I boiled it down once more and sold it as a two-line joke to [a humor magazine]."[15] In December 1926,

Helen finished her graduate work and returned home to New Jersey, where she began work as a teacher. Promising to never stray from each other for long, Ted booked passage on a boat back to America the following February.

## HOME AGAIN

Upon returning to America, Ted was out of money and decided to move back to Springfield. His parents were happy to have him home, but Ted wanted to be closer to Helen. During his brief time back in Springfield, he drew cartoons and submitted them to magazines in New York City. Elated by his first sale—to the *Saturday Evening Post* for $25—Ted packed his bags and moved to New York.

He rented an apartment, in the city's Greenwich Village district, with an old Dartmouth buddy and began what he hoped would be a lucrative career as a freelance cartoonist.

Throughout his life, Ted spoke of his powerful belief in luck and timing. He felt that the world provided windows of opportunity for everyone. By recognizing them and jumping through those windows at just the right time, people could achieve success. He was sure that his $25 sale was a clear signal for him to seek his fortune in New York.

## A Window Opens

Within weeks of being in New York, Ted got a job as a staff cartoonist for a magazine called *Judge*. It billed itself as the "world's wittiest weekly" and gave the former *Jacko* editor a starting salary of $75 a week.

Now that he had a steady job, he felt he could finally ask for Helen's hand in marriage. They were married on November 29, 1927, and moved in to an apartment across from a horse stable. Ted would later recall that it wasn't the nicest part of town. When a horse died in the stable, it would be dragged out into the street and left there for several days. The smell was horrible, but the little apartment was all they could afford.

In a letter written to his college friend Whit Campbell, Ted explained that the work he was producing for *Judge* was not of the same caliber as his earlier work because he had to simplify and water down his humor for the magazine's broad audience. In fact, Ted remembered receiving one of his very first pieces of "fan mail" from a Texas state penitentiary. It was from a man on death row who wasn't happy with the caliber of Geisel's work and wrote, "If your stuff is the kind of thing they're publishing nowadays, I don't so much mind leaving."[16]

With the onset of the Great Depression, *Judge* began experiencing financial problems and forced Ted to take a $25 per week salary cut. To make matters worse, sometimes they were unable to pay him even that and instead paid him in promotional products from their advertisers. On several occasions, he received cases of shaving cream and nail clippers in lieu of a paycheck.

Despite financial hardship, his experiences with *Judge* were of great value. He was given plenty of freedom to explore his creativity and often referred to his time there as his real graduate school. It's where he refined his talent for creating strange creatures—many of which would appear over and over again throughout his later works.

Among the milestones in his career at *Judge* was the creation of a cartoon series titled "Boids and Beasties." It was something of a precursor to Gary Larson's well-known Far Side comics. Since the cartoons were based on the biology and behavior of real animals, with a fictional humorous twist, Geisel decided to assume the identity of a fictional biologist. He signed these cartoons Dr. Theophrastus Seuss. He felt this would make up for the doctorate he never received at Oxford.

After this short-lived strip, he dropped the "Theophrastus," but the "Dr." remained for the rest of his life.

By far, the most significant event during his time at this magazine turned–graduate school was the creation of a sim-ple single-panel cartoon about a dragon, a knight, and a reference to a well-known insecticide of the day called Flit. The cartoon showed the knight lying in his bed and a dragon peering in on him. The caption underneath read, "Darn it all, another

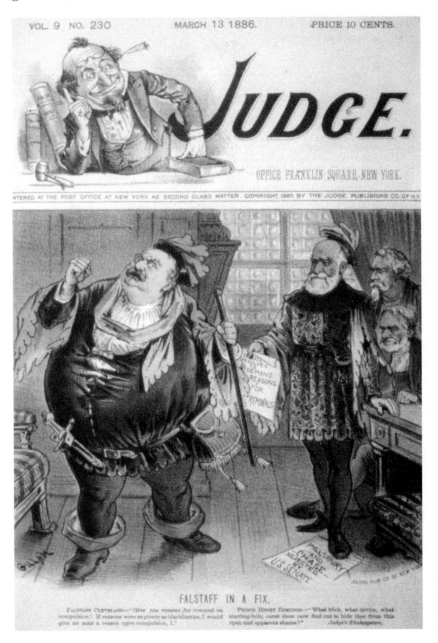

*Dr. Seuss was hired as a cartoonist for* Judge *where he began to hone his artistic skills.*

Dragon! And just after I'd sprayed the whole castle with Flit."[17]

A woman named Mrs. Lincoln Cleaves was reading his cartoon while waiting for her hair to dry at a salon and found it extremely funny. Mrs. Cleaves brought the cartoon to the attention of her husband, who was an advertising executive working on an account for Flit insecticide. She insisted that her husband contact the author of the cartoon and enlist his services for the ad campaign.

Mr. Cleaves first signed Geisel on for a few individual ads and was so pleased with his work that he decided to bring Ted on full-time. Geisel entered into a contract with Standard Oil, the parent company of Flit, and was paid $12,000 a year. This was a very large sum of money, especially since the country was in the grips of the Great Depression at the time. This stable income allowed Ted and Helen to move to a new apartment in a very posh section of New York, where, as Ted put it, "There were many fewer dead horses."[18]

This job would become a large part of Geisel's life. The Flit account afforded him not only money but fame as well. His continuous stream of Flit ads became known in every household throughout America. Each one featured a surreal buglike creature coming after someone, with a caption below that read, "Quick Henry, the Flit!" That catchphrase was as well known in the 1920s and '30s as Nike's "Just Do It" is today.

Geisel's work with Flit allowed him to get advertising work with a number of other companies, including the Ford Motor Company, NBC radio, and Holly Sugar. While his work at *Judge* continued, he also provided illustrations and humorous articles for magazines such as *Life* and *Vanity Fair*. At one point, his work even appeared on the cover of *Life* magazine. His career was soaring, and his very respectable salary allowed him to travel extensively to exotic places such as Turkey, Peru, Japan, and Africa.

## "SUCCESSFUL BUT FRUSTRATED"

Standard Oil recognized the gold it had discovered in Dr. Seuss and signed him to an exclusive contract. From then on, he could produce advertising work only for its subsidiaries. In addition to Flit, Standard Oil employed his services for Essolube Motor Oil and Essomarine boat fuel. His ad campaigns were everywhere, and he was making enough money to completely forget about the depression.

As lucrative and successful as his career was, he felt unfulfilled creatively. A man with the imagination of Dr. Seuss simply could not be happy working within the limited medium of advertising campaigns. He described himself as being "successful but frustrated."[19]

Finally, he discovered a loophole in his contract. He was not excluded from working on children's materials. So when Viking Press approached him to illustrate a British children's book, he accepted. The book, *Boners*, was released in 1931 and ended up on the *New York Times* nonfiction best-seller list. It was followed up with a sequel, *More Boners*, and Dr. Seuss's illustrations were cited as being a large

## THE SEUSS NAVY

*During Ted's early success in the advertising industry, he became something of a celebrity, known throughout the country for his clever "Quick Henry, the Flit" ad campaigns. In a 1960 article for the* New Yorker *magazine, E. J. Kahn discusses one of Dr. Seuss's early brushes with notoriety.*

"The firm that made Flit was a subsidiary of the Standard Oil Company of New Jersey, and every now and then he [Dr. Seuss] would be farmed out to another subsidiary, like the Essomarine fuel outfit. In this connection, he presided over a celebrated publicity stunt of the thirties—the Seuss Navy. The idea was spawned at the 1936 Motor Boat Show, and enrollment in the Navy was at first limited to owners of boats with inboard motors. Later, gossip columnists got in, some of them landlubbers [land lovers]. Every member was an admiral except Dr. Seuss, who was Admiral-in-Chief, and by 1940, when his Navy no longer seemed quite so funny, and petered out, it boasted a couple of thousand admirals. Its [banner] was a Geisel-designed herring, mostly bones, and its official seal was a flippered seal. Annually, at Motor Boat Show time, Essomarine picked up the tab for a Seuss Navy banquet, attended by nearly a thousand admirals, whom Geisel would sonorously [loudly] lead in an oath of allegiance to Mother Neptune—a mermaid-like creature he had rigged up out of a dressmaker's dummy and a fishtail. 'The Seuss Navy was a rather corny outfit,' Geisel says now."

factor in its success. One reviewer wrote, "Offhand . . . we should have said this would be a flop. But the [wonderful] illustrations of the renowned Dr. Seuss, of *Judge, Life,* and Flit fame, are not unlikely to put this over. They are simply swell."[20]

## THE MS *KUNGSHOLM*

Ted's success with *Boners* inspired him to further pursue the field of children's books. Not satisfied just to illustrate some-

one else's work, he decided to try his hand at writing as well. He put together a children's ABC book, with each letter illustrated with one of his bizarre creations. Not understanding much about the industry, he used so many inks in his drawings that the price of each book would have been astronomical. This idea was turned down by a number of publishers before Geisel abandoned it.

But again, fate would intervene. In the summer of 1936 Dr. Seuss and his wife took a cruise aboard the MS *Kungsholm*. The

*The ship's engines aboard the MS* Kungsholm *inspired Dr. Seuss to write his first children's book,* And to Think That I Saw It on Mulberry Street, *in anapestic tetrameter, a rhythmic device he used in most of his books.*

weather during their cruise was very bad and the guests were forced to stay below much of the time. Geisel retired to a bar in the depths of the ship and began jotting down the basic plot for a children's story:

> A stupid horse and wagon
> Horse and chariot
> Chariot pulled by Viking Ship
> Viking Ship sailing up a volcano
> Volcano blowing hearts, diamonds,
>     and clubs
> I saw a giant eight miles tall
> Who took the cards, 52 in all
> And played a game of solitaire.[21]

The churning rhythm of the ship's engines droned on and on in Ted's head. The repetitive sound of these engines created a beat to which he found himself repeating the phrase, "And that is a story that no one can beat, and to think that I saw it on Mulberry Street."[22] When he got home, he was still reciting this phrase in the ship's rhythm, and Helen convinced him to try putting it all together as a story.

## THE BEGINNING OF AN EMPIRE

After months of painstaking perfectionism, Ted finally completed the text and illustrations for *A Story That No One Can Beat* (as it was originally titled). He took it to a number of publishers, sure that he had a great success on his hands, but was met with rejection after rejection. After approaching twenty-seven publishers with no takers, he was ready to give up.

On his way home after the last one, he happened to run into Mike McClintock, an old Dartmouth friend. As luck would have it, McClintock had been promoted to juvenile editor of the publishing company Vanguard Press that day. This fortuitous meeting also happened to take place right in front of the Vanguard offices. McClintock offered to take a look at his book, and by the end of the day, after agreeing to change the title, Dr. Seuss had a contract for his first children's book, *And to Think That I Saw It on Mulberry Street.* This event reconfirmed Ted's belief in the power of luck and fate. That chance meeting with a friend he hadn't seen in years led to his launching one of the most successful children's book careers in history. Ted was later quoted as saying, "If I had been going down the other side of Madison Avenue, I'd be in the dry cleaning business today."[23]

## MULBERRY STREET

*And to Think That I Saw it on Mulberry Street* was a huge success when it was first released in 1937. It's the story of a boy named Marco who is bored by the ordinary sights he sees on the main street of his hometown. His father encourages him to keep his eyes open and see what there is to see on the way home from school each day. When confronted by the very ordinary sight of a plain horse and wagon, Marco creates a fantastic new reality centered around an ever-expanding circus parade that careens through the center of town. The simple horse and wagon are transformed, through the boy's imagination, into an amazing sight. When Marco arrives home, his father asks, "Was there nothing to look at . . . no people to greet? Did *nothing* excite you or make your heart beat?" Intimidated by his father's inquisition and perhaps afraid of getting in trouble for telling tall tales, Marco's reply is simply, " 'Nothing,' I said, growing red as a beet, 'But a plain horse and wagon on Mulberry Street.' "[24]

As with all of Dr. Seuss's books, critics have dissected the work to find the message it contains. Most seem to agree that it speaks to the idea that adults often impose their concept of reality onto children, quelling their imagination and creativity without even knowing it.

## ANAPESTIC TETRAMETER

What Geisel may or may not have known while creating this story down in the bowels of the MS *Kungsholm* was that the ship's engines were churning in anapestic tetrameter. This rhythmic device describes words that are put together in four groups of three syllables each, with the accent always going on the last syllable of the grouping. For example,

> Yes, the **Ze**bra is **fine**,
> But I **think** it's a **shame**,
> Such a **marvelous beast**
> With a **cart** that's so **tame**.[25]

This beat is what gives *Mulberry Street* its frantic pace and causes the reader to almost sing along with the text. It is also the

## THE JOKER

*Two of Ted's great loves were traveling and playing jokes on people. In the book,* Dr. Seuss and Mr. Geisel, *Judith and Neil Morgan describe his antics on a trip to Peru.*

"When they arrived at the harbor of Callao in 1934, a reporter from Lima's English-language newspaper expressed amazement that the Geisels had made the long journey to Peru two years in a row. Ted's imagination took over; on their first visit, he explained, he had suffered from altitude sickness at Cuzco, and since doctors had failed to find a way to control the 'headaches and insomnia of anoxemia,' he had undertaken his own research. Lining the walls of his Park Avenue studio with lead, he invented a device to pump air slowly out of the room until by the end of the winter he was 'living at an altitude of 19,000 feet' and 'enjoying superb health.' His return to Peru was a field test of his research.

On the next day the front-page headline in Lima read YANK SOLVES MYSTERY OF THE ANDES. 'Then my problem,' Ted recalled, 'was whether I should confess that it was a gag or go along with it. Everyone was curious, and I decided to go along. We got invitations to dinner at seven different embassies. One ambassador's wife almost did the dance of the seven veils to get the secret out of me. I didn't realize the whole economy of Peru was in the balance that year [and there was] trouble getting people to work in the mines because of altitude sickness.'"

device that Dr. Seuss would go on to use in most of his later books.

Again, luck had played a part in the future of Ted Geisel. Being stuck belowdecks with the maddening beating of those engines led to the birth and continued success of Dr. Seuss's signature style. In fact, an article published in *Time* magazine just after Geisel's death said of *Mulberry Street*, "The Seuss style was born fully developed: looping free-style drawings; clanging, infectious rhymes; and a relentless logic."[26] This completely unique style would propel Theodor Geisel into the limelight as the shining star of children's literature for the next fifty years.

# 3 An Explosive Career Begins

Riding on the success of *And to Think That I Saw It on Mulberry Street*, Dr. Seuss quickly produced a second book. *The 500 Hats of Bartholomew Cubbins* was a departure from what would come to be known as the more typical Seuss style. Rather than a rhyming circus of poetry married to images, *500 Hats* was more of a classic fairy tale, told in a narrative prose. Released in 1938, it too was an instant success.

## A NEW HOME

A young publisher at Random House named Bennett Cerf recognized Geisel's enormous talent. Cerf approached the writer and attempted to draw him out of his relationship with Vanguard Press. Random House was a much larger organization and could offer more than Vanguard in terms of marketing, creative freedom, and money. Geisel seemed to have an instant rapport with Cerf and took the offer. This deal marked the beginning of a life-long friendship and business relationship between the two men. Cerf had an enormous amount of respect for Geisel and was fond of telling people that, despite working with such authors as William Faulkner

and Eugene O'Neill, Ted Geisel was the only true genius currently working under the Random House banner.

Geisel was given complete freedom to develop his next project, and he decided

*Random House publisher Bennett Cerf (pictured) recognized Dr. Seuss's extraordinary artistic talents and gave him complete freedom on his first project.*

on an "adult" book. Released in 1939, *The Seven Lady Godivas* was another fairy tale. The story was about seven sisters, the seven men who came to court them, and the seven life lessons they learned in the process. This first book for Random House turned out to be Dr. Seuss's only complete commercial failure. Later in life, Dr. Seuss would claim that the book failed because he just couldn't get the people's knees right. He also stated in an interview with the *New Yorker* magazine in 1960, "I think maybe it all went to prove that I don't know anything about adults."[27]

Fortunately, Dr. Seuss's second project for Random House met with far more success. Later that same year, *The King's Stilts*

was published. Although not considered one of the classics in the Seuss library today, it was an engaging fairy tale about a king who needed to play in order to be an effective ruler. The following year, a more familiar character arrived on the scene: Horton the elephant. *Horton Hatches the Egg* came out in 1940 and was as big a success as his first two books. At last, Dr. Seuss was back on track.

On the heels of this success, however, came World War II, and Geisel's strong convictions about civic duty put his children's book career on hold for a few years. He enlisted in the army and didn't release another book until 1947. However, once back in the writing game, Dr. Seuss

Horton Hatches the Egg, *was Dr. Seuss's first big success at Random House.*

proceeded to plow through the decades with an uninterrupted string of successful projects. From *McElligot's Pool*, which gained him his first Caldecott Honor, and the return of Horton in *Horton Hears a Who!* to such later classics as *Yertle the Turtle* and *Green Eggs and Ham*, there seemed to be no limit to his creativity or appeal.

## THE DOCTOR'S APPEAL

Over the years, many critics and literary authorities have tried to decipher Dr. Seuss's formula for success. Occupying five of the top fifteen slots in *Publisher Weekly*'s list of the all-time best-selling children's books, he is by far the most well known children's author to date, with forty-seven published books and more than 200 million copies sold. What was it that made his work so appealing to so many people? It may have a lot to do with the fact that he was, in many ways, a child himself. He refused to grow up and buy into what he called the adult conspiracy—his notion that grown-ups covertly seek to strip the world of its creativity and suppress the ideas of children. Dr. Seuss was often quoted as saying that his success could be attributed to the fact that he didn't write for kids, he wrote for people.

An article in the *New York Times*, however, stated that he simply won audiences over "by the sneaky stratagem of making them laugh."[28] His ability to bring a smile to the face of any man, woman, or child probably had a lot to do with his success. Dr. Seuss also felt that adults tend to get bogged down in the day-to-day accountabilities of life and then impose this habit on children. He encouraged people, young and old, to find amusement in the ordinary nuts and bolts of life. By creating something extraordinary out of even the most boring situation, his characters show people that rollicking fun is simply a state of mind. However, to keep his farce in a tightly wrapped package, he pursued this belief with a painstaking attention to detail.

## LOGICAL INSANITY

On a number of occasions, Dr. Seuss talked about the logical insanity that pervaded his books. He believed that, to make his outlandish stories and characters believable, they should be fixed in a framework that has the appearance of reality. During an interview with *Life* magazine, he described this logical insanity as the

> simple premise that children will believe a ludicrous situation if pursued with relentless logic. If I start with a two-headed animal I must never waver from that concept. There must be two hats in the closet, two toothbrushes in the bathroom and two sets of spectacles on the night table.[29]

This grounded structuring of the fantasy world makes it seem more real to children and allows them to identify with the character and be drawn into the world Dr. Seuss has created. For example, one of his more surreal books, *McElligot's Pool*, has to do with a boy who is fishing in a small pool of water in the middle of nowhere. The book, which is one of Dr. Seuss's

# THE END OF LAUGHTER

*One of the reasons often quoted for the success of Dr. Seuss's books is the fact that he truly seemed to understand what makes children laugh. In 1952, he wrote an article for the* New York Times Book Review *discussing his philosophy on the difference between adults' and children's senses of humor. Dr. Seuss believed that the child's sense of humor is natural, while the adult's is conditioned, or trained.*

"[As a child] you [people] saw life through very clear windows. Small windows, of course, but very bright windows. And then, what happened? You know what happened. The grown-ups began to equip you with shutters. . . . They decided your humor was crude and too primitive. You were laughing too loud, too often and too happily. It was time you learned to laugh with a little more restraint. . . . Your young unfettered mind, they told you, was taking you on too many wild flights of fancy. It was time your imagination got its feet down on the ground. It was time your version of humor was given a practical realistic base. . . . And the process of destroying your spontaneous laughter was under way. . . . [Adults exhibit] conditioned laughter [which] doesn't spring from [any] juices. It doesn't even spring. Conditioned laughter germinates like toadstools on a stump."

*Dr. Seuss's books appeal to children's sense of humor and, in turn, their primitive ability to laugh without restraint.*

greatest achievements in illustration, shows all the fantastic types of fish that might inhabit that ocean. These fish, while simply the product of the boy's overactive imagination, are made to seem real, as they are based on small bits of reality that have been exaggerated or distorted. The Eskimo fish, for example, has an Eskimo's face. The jellyfish is pink because, according to the text, it is full of strawberry jelly. The catfish, which looks more like a cat than a fish, is chased by a creature looking much like a dog.

Even the silliness of Dr. Seuss's vocabulary is made more credible by this unbroken stream of logical insanity. At the end of *Horton Hears a Who!* the miniature town is saved by the exclamation of its tiniest resident, young Jo-Jo, who lets out a resounding "YOP!" This word is unfamiliar to the young reader and would seem too foreign to use as the climax to the story if not for the groundwork set earlier on. The first sound Horton hears from the speck is a "yelp." Later an eagle tells him to quit his yapping, and even the mayor of the little city explains that the townspeople are yapping and yipping, doing their best to be heard. So in the end, it seems sensible for the world-saving word to be a nonsensical "YOP!" It is this minute and pervasive attention to detail that makes the insanity of a Dr. Seuss story as acceptable as events in the real world.

*The world's most well-known children's author, Dr. Seuss has sold more than 200 million copies of his books.*

## FAST-PACED FUN

Another explanation for the popularity of Dr. Seuss's books has to do with their pace.

Anapestic tetrameter gives the text a flowing, almost musical quality. It encourages the reader to be carried away with the flow of the story. This ride, however, is not a steady one. The pace of most Dr. Seuss books starts out slowly and then builds.

One literary critic, Selma Lanes, has likened this pace to blowing up a balloon, adding tension and size with each successive breath. Lanes claims that Dr. Seuss intentionally builds the pace with an ever-increasing velocity; the story gets bigger and grander, the pictures more colorful and elaborate. The tension builds and readers are nearly overwhelmed by the text and images until they feel they can take it no longer. Just as the reader is nearly wincing with anticipation of what will come next, the story usually ends not with a bang but a whimper. Dr. Seuss hits the pressure release valve and, as suddenly as it took off, the story ends. Often, it returns to the starting point, where reality resurfaces and the action is completely diffused.

*And to Think That I Saw It on Mulberry Street* is a perfect illustration of this. Marco starts out by simply transforming a horse-drawn wagon into a zebra-drawn wagon. With the turn of each page, the Mulberry Street procession gets larger and more elaborate. By the end of the story, every inch of the page is covered with color. There are planes, confetti, a grandstand, a police escort, giraffes, a magician, and even a small house being towed along. Just as the reader begins to experience sensory overload, and is almost wary of turning the page, it all comes to a crashing halt. The simple image of the horse and wagon reappears, as Marco tells his father that there was nothing to see.

## THE POWER OF IMAGINATION

Although Marco's grand parade disappeared at the close of the story, there is no doubt that, for at least a time, it seemed very real to him. His imagination was that strong, and perhaps the most central and important theme throughout all of Dr. Seuss's books is the concept of imagina-

tion. Geisel firmly believed that a rich imagination was one of the most important possessions in life. He said,

> I like nonsense, it wakes up the brain cells. Fantasy is a necessary ingredient in living, it's a way of looking at life through the wrong end of a telescope. Which is exactly what I do, and that enables you to laugh at life's realities.[30]

Many of his books, such as *If I Ran the Circus*, *Mulberry Street*, and *McElligot's Pool* project the message that there are an infinite number of ways to look at reality and the world. Exploring one's creativity can help solve even the most overwhelming challenges in life.

In his own life, Dr. Seuss had experienced the importance of creativity. He witnessed his father's ability to reinvent himself and find a whole new career path, and Geisel himself had successfully used creativity to convince people to buy insecticides and other products. In books like *If I Ran the Zoo*, these links to his personal experiences can be clearly seen.

Geisel's father used his ingenuity to make great improvements to the local Springfield Zoo, gaining the respect and praise of the local townspeople. Almost a childlike version of Dr. Seuss's father, *If I Ran the Zoo*'s young Gerald McGrew enters the local zoo and sees it as drab and uninteresting. He begins to imagine the incredible animals he would bring in if he ran the zoo. From elephant-cats to Gussets, Gherkins, and Gaskets, Gerald imagines a full encyclopedia of fantastic creatures. *If I Ran the Zoo* clearly encourages young readers to shed the boundaries of the world around them and see where it takes them.

As McGrew brings in wilder and wilder animals, he is greeted with success and the adulation of the zoo guests. At first, the praise is simple, but it continues to grow and, by the end, he envisions his efforts bringing him near-legendary fame. Dr. Seuss wrote,

> The whole *world* will say, "Young
> McGrew's made his mark.
> He's built a zoo better than Noah's
> whole Ark!
> These wonderful, marvelous beasts
> that he chooses
> Have made him the greatest of all the
> McGrewses!"[31]

Again, Dr. Seuss doesn't just preach a concept but demonstrates it through his ability to marry words to images. He takes the reader along for a joyride, bringing these unusual animals to life. For example, the image of the tizzle-topped Tufted Mazurka is really just a colorful bird with a long neck. However, as one reads the words that describe it, the drawing seems to become more fantastic. Dr. Seuss wrote,

> I'll go to the African island of Yerka
> And bring back a tizzle-topped
> Tufted Mazurka,
> A kind of canary with quite a tall
> throat.
> His neck is so long, if he swallows an
> oat

## THE BIG BALLOON

*In her book* Down the Rabbit Hole, *quoted in* Of Sneetches and Whos and the Good Dr. Seuss, *Selma G. Lanes analyzes Dr. Seuss's work and talks about the "inflating balloon" technique he uses in his stories.*

"Seuss has managed, almost single-handedly, to provide a safety valve for the overscheduled, overburdened and overstimulated child of modern civilization. In recognizing that children's craving for excitement, in their books as in their lives, is often merely the means for releasing pent-up anxiety, Seuss cannily manages to magnify and multiply the sense of suspense in his stories, not so much by the ingenuity of his plots as by a clever and relentless piling on of gratuitous anxiety until the child is fairly ready to cry 'uncle' and settle for any resolution, however mundane, that will end his at once marvelous, exquisite and finally unbearable tension. The process is not unlike the blowing up of a balloon: bigger, bigger, bigger and finally, when the bursting point is reached, Seuss simply releases his grip and all tension, like trapped air, is freed."

For breakfast the first day of April, they say
It has to go down such a very long way
That it gets to his stomach the fifteenth of May.[32]

Dr. Seuss doesn't just describe the new and exotic beasts but rounds out the story and young Gerald's imaginative prowess by creating wild places of origin for many of the creatures, such as Hippo-No-Hungus, the mountains of Tobsk, and the island of Gwark. He also creates strange devices to ensnare the animals, such as the Skeegle-Mobile and the Bad-Animal-Catching-Machine. Dr. Seuss's imagination appears limitless and, through it, he inspires children. He encourages them to shed the rules and boundaries that the world imposes on them and explore their own creativity.

## WHERE FANTASY AND SCIENCE MEET

Creating fantasy worlds and situations gave Dr. Seuss a perfect venue for his talents and served the very real function of entertaining readers. Some would argue that his books served a higher purpose as

*Dr. Seuss holds a sculpture of one of the unusual, imaginary animals that came to life in his books.*

## WORTHWHILE FANTASY

*In "On Beyond Zebra with Dr. Seuss" in the fall 1989 issue of the* New Advocate, *journalist Rita Roth discusses the importance of fantasy in Dr. Seuss's works and the message this sends children.*

"Because these stories call into question ideologies that reinforce the established society, they illustrate the view that the way things are is not necessarily how they must be. What meanings could children take from this perspective? These delightfully zany tales provide children an alternative voice, a voice that turns away from passive conformity and encourages active engagement and a sense of community."

well. An article by Chet Raymo in the *Horn Book*, a children's literature journal, credited books like Dr. Seuss's as being responsible for creating the next generation of scientists and explorers. Raymo argued that imagination is the most crucial element that a scientist must possess. A mind, he said, that is truly open to any and all possibilities is able to think on a higher level, to see possibilities where others cannot. These are the people who reinvent science and technology and remain at the cutting edge of their field. According to Raymo, "To be a scientist . . . one must be like the kid in Dr. Seuss' *On Beyond Zebra!* who refused to be limited by the fact of the alphabet: 'In the Places I go there are things that I see/That I *never* could spell if I stopped with the Z.'"[33]

*On Beyond Zebra!* was an early poke at the practices of the traditional academic community. Dr. Seuss felt that by focusing on rote memorization of facts and instilling the notion of success through conformity, schools often stifled true exploration and imagination. In this story, a young boy shows off his academic achievements to an older friend by demonstrating his mastery of the alphabet. The older boy explains that he has not yet begun to learn, because the "real" alphabet doesn't end with Z. "I'm telling you this 'cause you're one of my friends. *My* alphabet starts where *your* alphabet ends!"[34] The older boy becomes an explorer of sorts, likening himself to Christopher Columbus. He takes the younger boy on an elephant's back, in a gondola, and even in a spaceship to show him the amazing things that can be spelled with the letters after Z. The message here seems to be that anything is possible once people move beyond the conventions of what they are told is reality.

## EMPOWERMENT

Another recurring theme in Dr. Seuss books is the power of the underdog. Geisel felt very strongly about bullies—both of the schoolyard and political variety. This feeling may have originated from his early childhood experience of being

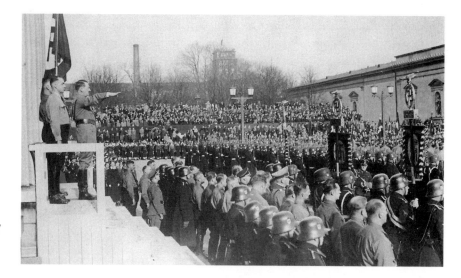

*Yertle the Turtle, a book featuring a turtle who rose to power on the backs of other turtles, was inspired by the rise of Hitler in Germany.*

persecuted by other children because of his German ancestry. Whatever the reason, it is clear from his books and political cartoons that he held the concept of oppressing the powerless in disdain.

Ever the child advocate, Geisel saw children as another group suffering from the oppression of a dictatorial institution—adults. He was often quoted as saying that he treated children as equals and believed others should as well. Many of his works deal with the concept of empowering the helpless. In his books, heroism exists in ordinary people (or creatures). Ruth K. Mac-Donald, a professor of children's literature, agreed saying, "Empowering children and encouraging mastery and independence is one of the central themes in all of Dr. Seuss' works."[35]

## A FASCIST TURTLE

One of Dr. Seuss's shortest and most popular stories has to do with oppression and empowerment. *Yertle the Turtle* is an allegory about an over-reaching turtle king who, according to Dr. Seuss, was modeled after the rise of Hitler. This tyrannical terrapin is the ruler of all that he sees, but he wants to rule more than just a simple little pond. He decides that the more he can see, the more he can rule and orders his subjects to stack themselves up high enough so that he can climb on their backs and see what else is out there. Dr. Seuss wrote,

> "All mine!" Yertle cried, "Oh, the
> things I now rule!
> I'm king of a cow! And I'm king of a
> mule!
> I'm king of a house! And, what's
> more, beyond that,
> I'm king of a blueberry bush and a
> cat!
> I'm Yertle the turtle! Oh, marvelous
> me!
> For I am the ruler of all that I see!"[36]

Yertle continues to demand more turtles to stand on. As he rises higher and higher and his thirst for power grows stronger and stronger, one small turtle on the bottom finally speaks up and complains that his back hurts. Enraged, Yertle orders him to be silent. This lowliest of turtles, who seems to represent the voice of the pond's subjects, continues to groan and gripe. Eventually, he does a very simple thing. He burps. With that one burp, Yertle is toppled from his overextended throne and crashes to the pond below. The story ends with,

> And the turtles, of course . . . all the
> turtles are free
> As turtles and, maybe, all creatures
> should be.[37]

## NEVER A STRAIGHT ANSWER

Although Dr. Seuss may have admitted the source of his inspiration for *Yertle the Turtle*, he was not always so straightforward. Over the years, many interviewers asked him where he got all his great ideas. His responses ranged from the plausible to the surreal. He told one interviewer that he traveled to the Arizona desert and picked the brain of a retired "thunderbird," although he denied having any idea where the bird got its ideas. Another time he told someone that each year he traveled to a small town in Switzerland called Zybilknov to get his cuckoo clock fixed. While waiting for the clock, he walked the streets of the village and talked to the inhabitants, gleaning ideas from them.

A journalist with *Life* magazine once asked him how he created all the unusual names for his exotic lands and creatures. Dr. Seuss responded, "Why, I've been to most of these places myself so the names are from memory. As for the animals, I have a special dictionary which gives most of them, and I just look up the spellings."[38] Geisel's first wife, Helen, claimed that he simply had the unbridled imagination of a child. In that same *Life* magazine interview, she said, "His mind has never grown up."[39] Apparently, the creativity Dr. Seuss demonstrated in his books had a place in his personal life as well.

## THE WORLD TRAVELER

Upon further investigation, it appears that some of Dr. Seuss's ideas did come from real-life experiences. He took at least some of his inspiration from his extensive travels around the world. Geisel loved to travel and constantly took notes on the people, places, and animals he saw. He said,

> I've loved animals for as long as I can remember. The first thing I do when I am travelling is to visit the nearest zoo. It's a wonder that after all the animals I've seen I can't make them true to life. When I do an elephant, the poor beast usually winds up with not only too many joints in his legs but with too many legs.[40]

The inspiration for *The 500 Hats of Bartholomew Cubbins*, for example, came to Geisel while sitting on a commuter train in 1937. Dr. Seuss said, "There was a very stiff broker sitting in front of me. I wondered what his reaction would be if I took his hat off and threw it out the window. I decided that he was so stuffy he would grow a new one."[41]

## UBER GLETCH

*In the fall of 1989 Dr. Seuss was interviewed for an article in the* Horn Book. *He was asked where he comes up with his story ideas and, as usual he offered a creative response.*

"This is the most asked question of any successful author. Most authors will not disclose their source for fear that other less successful authors will chisel in on their territory. However, I am willing to take a chance. I get all my ideas in Switzerland near the Forka Pass. There is a little town called Gletch, and two thousand feet up above Gletch there is a smaller hamlet called Uber Gletch. I go there on the fourth of August every summer to get my cuckoo clock repaired. While the cuckoo is in the hospital, I wander around and talk to the people in the streets. They are very strange people, and I get my ideas from them."

In an interview for *Parenting* magazine, Geisel admitted that he got the idea for *Horton Hears a Who!* while on assignment for a magazine in Japan. He was dismayed by the American anti-Japanese sentiment after World War II. After spending time among the Japanese people, he realized that they were intensely proud and optimistic. Their government was making valiant attempts to reconstruct the country by attempting to enlist the support of every citizen and encouraging everyone to vote and get involved.

The "Whos" in *Horton Hears a Who!* were apparently modeled after the Japanese. The Whos are seen as small and insignificant, scorned by the other members of the jungle and desperate to save themselves from obliteration.

Not all of Dr. Seuss's ideas came from his globe-spanning travels, however. The genesis of *Horton Hatches the Egg* was far

less exotic. Geisel left some drawings out on his desk near an open window one day and when he returned to work, the wind had blown the transparencies on top of one another. Dr. Seuss found that a drawing of an elephant had landed on top of another drawing of a tree in such a way that it looked like the elephant was sitting *in* the tree. Geisel remembered being amused by the image and turning it into a story. He said, "All I had to do was figure out what the hell that elephant was doing in that tree, and I had a book."[42]

By the early 1950s, Geisel's life had taken him in many different directions. He had traveled the world, gained success and financial reward in the advertising business, served his country in World War II, and become a very well-known children's author. However, with all these achievements behind him, his greatest success was still to come.

# 4 The Cat Who Taught Kids to Read

For the first twenty years of Dr. Seuss's children's book career, he managed to produce an amazing string of successes. From his first attempt with *And to Think That I Saw It on Mulberry Street* to such classics as *Horton Hears a Who!* and *If I Ran the Zoo*, Dr. Seuss gained praise from his peers, critics, and the general public. However, it was not until 1957, at the age of fifty-three, that he created his most famous and lasting success. The publication of *The Cat in the Hat* launched his already booming career into the stratosphere, and put into motion a chain of events that would forever secure his position as, according to one reviewer, "the undisputed king of the kiddies' end of the bookshelf."[43]

## AS LUCK WOULD HAVE IT

*The Cat in the Hat* came about through a very circuitous turn of events. It all began in 1956 when John Hersey wrote an article for *Life* magazine titled "Why Johnny Can't Read." Hersey explained that much of America's youth was having great difficulty learning to read. In his opinion, these problems could be traced back to the ineffective "Dick and Jane" primers, or first

books, that children were given in early grade school. Hersey claimed that the primers were painfully boring and made learning to read an unpleasant chore from the outset. He explained that when children have fun and demonstrate a passion for something, they have a much easier time learning. In an offhand comment, Hersey suggested that someone like Dr. Seuss should write a children's reading primer. William Spaulding, the educational director at Houghton Mifflin publishers, saw this article and contacted Ted Geisel.

## HARDER THAN IT SOUNDS

Geisel was very excited about the project. After some lengthy contract negotiations, the publishers decided that Houghton Mifflin would distribute the book to libraries and schools, while Random House, Geisel's longtime publisher, would retain the rights to market it in the public sector.

Geisel was given a list of about 250 words and told that it was the standard list from which a reading primer must be written. It was explained to him that very young children had a specific set of small words they could recognize and that he

The Cat In the Hat, *written as a children's reading primer, met with unprecedented commercial success.*

must only use words from this list to write his book. Accustomed to working in a medium of unbridled creativity, often making up his own words, Dr. Seuss had great difficulty working within such limited guidelines. Initially thinking the project would take him just a few weeks, he ended up spending more than nine months on it.

Perhaps his biggest challenge was simply finding a place to start. He could not think of a title or a solid idea from which to begin. Finally, in desperation, he decided that he would take the first two words on the list that rhymed and use them for the title. Those words were *cat* and *hat*. After many months of struggling, in the spring of 1957 one of the world's most famous children's books was finally born.

## THE CAT TAKES FLIGHT

Despite its problematic creation, *The Cat in the Hat* met with unprecedented success in the commercial market from the day it arrived on the bookshelves. Dr. Seuss's other books had been successful, but nothing had prepared him for this. To put it in perspective, at that time *Horton Hatches the Egg*, one of his larger commercial successes, had sold about 200,000 copies—after being in print for twenty years. *The Cat in the Hat* passed the 1 million mark in its first two years of publication. And although Dr. Seuss had been getting a steady flow of fan mail for more than a decade, Random House reported that in 1957 alone, after the release of *The Cat in the Hat*, he received more than four and a half tons of mail.

Geisel was overwhelmed by the book's success. He spent the next two years traveling the country on a nonstop promotional tour. His publisher had him booked for appearances everywhere—from local bookstores to major universities to national

---

### NOT EVERYONE LOVES CATS

*Although it was a huge commercial success when it was first published, many educators refused to see* The Cat in the Hat *as a serious learning tool. As the years passed, however, its value in the classroom became more apparent. In an article for the* New Advocate *titled "On Beyond Zebra with Dr. Seuss," schoolteacher Rita Roth recalls how her attitude changed over time.*

"I remember feeling puzzled [and] a little annoyed by the strong preference my students showed for Dr. Seuss. However, there was no way I could ignore their enthusiasm as they read and reread *The Cat in the Hat*. . . . Whatever the reason for his attraction, it seemed clear to me then that Dr. Seuss, like comic books, provided a kind of frivolity that was not appropriate for school. 'Let the children read Dr. Seuss at home,' I thought, 'not in my classroom.' Still, there was no denying the impact of his work and its popularity. I wondered who this Dr. Seuss was and why children were perennially tuned-in to his tales. Twenty years later, I teach children's literature, language arts, and reading to teachers and prospective teachers. With a less narrow view of what constitutes school language learning and a wider base of experience, I find Dr. Seuss more than a peddler of mere nonsense. Geisel deserves serious attention because his work is replete with social commentary and critique. . . . [His] stories present useful insights into our culture and the experience of childhood."

---

television talk shows. Uncomfortable with public appearances since the days of his early childhood, Geisel grimly agreed to the demands placed on him.

Not all the success was unwelcomed, however. Just three years before *The Cat in the Hat*, Dr. Seuss had called his agent, Phyllis Jackson, to ask if he could count on book royalties of at least $5,000 that year. He was concerned that he and Helen would be unable to make ends meet. By 1959, he was taking in an annual salary of about $200,000, making him the world's highest paid author of that year.

## WHY A CAT?

Many critics have looked for an answer to the question Why was this book so enormously successful? *The Cat in the Hat* wasn't so different from other Dr. Seuss

*Dr. Seuss confers with his wife Helen at their home in La Jolla, California, 1957. Two years later, he became the highest paid author of the year.*

books; at its core, it is simply a fun ride through a colorful landscape of words and images. One critic, Mary Lystad, feels it may be because the book seems to sum up Dr. Seuss's whole attitude toward life. She says, "The message is clear—if the world is bleak, change it, create a new world!"[44]

*The Cat in the Hat* is the story of two children who are stuck at home, bored. Suddenly, a cat arrives and turns their whole world upside down. From the cat's initial, flamboyant appearance, he provides the children, and the reader, with a much-needed escape. He doesn't simply promise them fun but declares that they will have "fun that is funny."[45] This speaks to Dr. Seuss's notion that adults' perception of what is funny, which they often try to impose on children, is often drab and lacking true hilarity. Through this statement, the cat promises to break this mold—much like the book promises to break the mold of current reading primers—and give the children a solid raucous belly-laugh. As usual, Dr. Seuss delivers.

Ruth MacDonald believes that the book is nearly irresistible to many children because it invites them into a forbidden conspiracy of fun. With the exception of the mother's foot and hand coming through the front door at the end of the book, the entire story takes place in the absence of any adults. There is widespread mayhem going on in the house, the kind of destructive fun that is strictly forbidden in most homes. The children in the story are equally enthralled and appalled by the cat's antics. MacDonald suggests that the children in the book are seen as "innocent bystanders," which allows the child reader to identify with them without feeling guilty at having done something wrong.

Adults seem to love the book as well. Geisel felt strongly that it was up to parents, not just teachers, to instill a love of reading in their children. "Teaching a child to read," he said, "is a family setup. It's the business of having books around the house, not forcing them. Parents should have twenty books stacked on tables or set around the living room. The average kid will pick one up, find something interesting. And pretty soon he's reading."[46]

Furthermore, Geisel believed that being forced to read to a child can sometimes be even more tiresome for the parent than the child. Often toddlers have a favorite story that they insist on hearing over and over. A success on many levels, *The Cat in the Hat* kept most adults from getting burned out on reading to their children. For perhaps the first time ever, reading at home was seen as a fun activity for the entire family.

## No Cats Allowed (In School)

Although Random House was extremely pleased with the sales of *The Cat in the Hat* in the public sector, Houghton Mifflin was gravely disappointed. Not only didn't the book take off as well in libraries and classrooms as it did in the bookstores, but it actually met with quite a bit of professional resistance. Many educators shunned the book and refused to take it seriously as a learning tool. One reason for this boycott may have had to do with simple pride. Some educators did not like the fact that

*Wisconsin senator Chuck Chvala reads to a group of interested children. Dr. Seuss wanted his books to be both fun and instructive.*

Seuss used the title of "Dr." when he hadn't earned it. This may have labeled him as something of a charlatan to people who had spent many years working very hard to earn their doctorates.

A more common sentiment, however, had to do with the frivolous nature of *The Cat in the Hat*. Teachers felt that education was a serious matter and that the book was just too silly to be taken seriously. An article in *New Yorker* magazine in 1960 explained that many educators "felt that the teaching process is a solemn business, not to be interrupted by avoidable laughter."[47]

Other teachers felt that, in an effort to undo the stuffiness of the "Dick and Jane" readers, Dr. Seuss overcompensated and created a book that instructs children to be destructive and shun authority. Dr. Seuss, however, was quick to point out that *The Cat in the Hat* was never meant to be an instruction manual for appropriate play behavior. He said, "Most every child learning to read has problems, and I am just saying to them that reading is fun."[48]

Apparently, this message got across. In a 1989 article for the *New Advocate*, schoolteacher Rita Roth discussed how her opinion of Dr. Seuss changed gradually over time. Overwhelmed by *The Cat in the Hat*'s popularity with her students year after year, she felt obligated to reevaluate its worth and found it to be a surprisingly effective tool for early readers. Eventually, *The Cat in the Hat,* along with the books that would follow, became an accepted and even cherished part of the professional teaching establishment. Roth may have summed it up best when she said, "[Dr. Seuss] has become as common a part of elementary classrooms as crayons."[49]

## THE NEXT GENERATION

According to one literary critic, "*The Cat in the Hat* liquidated Dick and Jane forever,"[50] meaning it changed the way teachers taught and students learned. Following *The Cat in the Hat*, Geisel decided to expand its success and use it to help him fulfill a personal goal. He had always wanted to be an educator but never had

the patience to sit through formal graduate school. Geisel had clearly demonstrated over the years, and most clearly with *The Cat in the Hat*, that he understood how to communicate effectively with children. He seemed to have an uncanny ability to understand how their minds processed information and he was inspired to use that talent to help educate children on a larger scale. As a result, Geisel established a new branch of Random House Books called Beginner Books. Through this company, he wrote and oversaw a full line of entertaining educational materials designed to help teach children to read.

Over the next thirty years, Dr. Seuss wrote twenty-two Beginner Books, including such well-known titles as *Hop on Pop*, *Fox in Socks*, *Green Eggs and Ham*, and *The Cat in the Hat Comes Back*. In addition to the books he wrote himself, he oversaw the production of a number of Beginner Books by other authors, including Jan and Stan Berenstain, who wrote the *Berenstain*

---

### THE COMPLEX SOCK

*Geisel often talked about the complexity of writing his seemingly simple stories. He describes this in an excerpt from Jonathan Cott's book* Pipers at the Gates of Dawn.

"The difficult thing about writing in verse for kids is that you can write yourself into a box: If you can't get a proper rhyme for a [stanza], you not only have to throw that [stanza] out but you also have to unravel the sock way back, probably ten pages or so. . . . You find that you're not driving the car, your *characters* are driving it. And you also have to remember that in a children's book a paragraph is like a chapter in an adult book, and a sentence is like a paragraph."

*Bear* books. On some occasions he even collaborated with other illustrators. In these instances, he wrote the text and someone else provided the drawings. The reasons for these collaborations ranged from his having too many commitments in a given year to his assertion that some books simply called for more realistic drawings than he was able to produce. Whatever the reason, when Geisel wrote a Beginner Book with someone else, it was published under the name of Theo. LeSieg (Geisel spelled backwards).

All Beginner Books, whether written by Dr. Seuss or someone else, followed the same basic principles. They were designed to show a relationship between pictures and text, to introduce written words using visual clues as to their meanings. This technique demonstrates that letters and words are not part of a picture but a caption that describes the picture.

## How to Make Reading Fun

The language in all these books involves words that commonly exist in a child's world, such as simple household items, body parts, and activities. However, one of the first things Geisel did after *The Cat in the Hat* was to get rid of the rigid word list that had caused him so much trouble. The words would remain simple, but never limited. He didn't believe in the notion that there were only 250 words the average five- or six-year-old could read. He stated in an interview with *U.S. News & World Report,* "I changed the rules, based on my belief that a child could learn any amount of words if fed them slowly and if the books were amply illustrated."[51]

In addition to illustrations, a number of devices are used in each Beginner Book to make it a good tool for learning. The plots are always simple and straightforward. There is never any text that is not pictured in an illustration, and there is never more than one basic illustration per page. Easier words always come first, followed by larger, more difficult words that build on the child's earlier successes. The pages often end in cliffhangers, encouraging readers to go on. Also, the emphasis for the anapestic tetrameter is often highlighted with capital letters to help the child follow the flow. Furthermore, words are repeated whenever possible. For example, at the end of *The Cat in the Hat*, the mess in the house is rapidly cleaned up by the cat's strange machine, allowing Dr. Seuss to re-cap all the objects that were disturbed throughout the story. The books also steer the child's pronunciation of words that may be more difficult to sound out at first sight by pairing them in rhyme with other easier words.

## Lady Luck Comes to Breakfast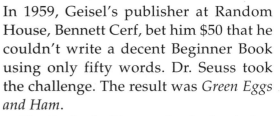

In 1959, Geisel's publisher at Random House, Bennett Cerf, bet him $50 that he couldn't write a decent Beginner Book using only fifty words. Dr. Seuss took the challenge. The result was *Green Eggs and Ham*.

*The Cat in the Hat* may be the book that Dr. Seuss is most well-known for, but it is

*Throughout his life, Ted Geisel demanded a nearly unattainable level of perfection from himself. In most cases he sweated laboriously over every word and picture in his books. This excerpt from an article in the December 1960 issue of the* New Yorker *describes the process.*

"Being harshly self-critical, Geisel at one point or another in the evolution of each of his books has hurled his accumulated words and pictures onto the floor or into a fireplace, whence they are customarily retrieved by his wife and restored to his hands when he's in a less [irritable] mood. Perfectionism is his creed. He insists on retyping a page of copy if one word has been crossed out, and he has spent up to three days worrying about the appositeness [appropriateness] of a single adjective."

actually *Green Eggs and Ham* that holds the title of his best-seller. It has sold more than 6 million copies and is number seven on *Publisher Weekly*'s most recent list of the best-selling children's books ever written. In fact, a poll by the National Education Association conducted in the year 2000 asked eighteen hundred schoolchildren to rank their favorite books and the forty-year-old *Green Eggs and Ham* came in third after such contemporary favorites as J. K. Rowling's Harry Potter books and R. L. Stine's Goosebumps series.

The popularity of *Green Eggs and Ham* can be attributed to its simplicity and universal appeal. It's a fun story, full of fast-paced action, which elevates the "inflating balloon" device to new heights. Almost every child in the world can associate with either the pestering Sam or his friend who steadfastly refuses to try new and unusual foods.

From an educational point of view, it is also a great achievement. The book is based on very simple words that are cumulatively repeated until, by the end, the child has a firm grasp on all fifty of them. The response to this simple book spawned an even simpler idea.

## WHAT COLOR IS YOUR FISH?

*One Fish Two Fish Red Fish Blue Fish* is technically listed as a Beginner Book, but it was actually an early attempt at something far simpler. According to Geisel, "It's a book based on an educational theory I have, but one I unfortunately can't define."[52] He would later describe it as a prebeginner book.

*One Fish Two Fish* attempts to introduce toddlers to the concept of the written word. Geared toward an even younger age bracket than regular Beginner Books, it tries to convey the idea that printed words are symbols or representations of objects, people, actions, or situations. It

*Children from Winthrop Elementary School, in New London, Connecticut, listen to* One Fish Two Fish Red Fish Blue Fish, *another popular reading primer by Dr. Seuss.*

does this by neatly placing every word or phrase in the text right next to the object it describes. Children who have never been taught about words or reading are able to go back to the book, once it has been read to them, and identify the familiar words all by themselves, using the pictures as a guide. The book was well received at the time, and many critics applauded Dr. Seuss's efforts to introduce reading to a younger generation than ever thought possible.

Though exciting to some, this was an unwelcome achievement to others. In the days before preschool was the norm,

some educators felt that the toddler years were too early to burden young minds with the concept of reading. Geisel's answer to such alarmists was, as usual, both pointed and amusing. He announced that he "may someday facilitate pre-natal reading, by inventing a 250 word pill that expectant mothers can swallow."[53]

## YET ANOTHER LINE

After experimenting with *One Fish Two Fish Red Fish Blue Fish*, Geisel was convinced that there was a need for even more prebeginner books. He said that "Adults minimize the speed and the desire children have for learning. Children can do at three or four what is expected from them at six or seven."[54]

The result was the creation of yet another line, called Bright and Early Books. These books were geared toward an even younger audience than the Beginner Books and much like *One Fish Two Fish* they simply introduce the concept of the written word. Dr. Seuss explained the series as "an attempt to initiate very young children into the mysteries of reading by seeing to it that almost every word in the text is neatly juxtaposed with an illustration of the object it describes."[55]

Starting with *The Foot Book* in 1968, Dr. Seuss wrote a total of twelve Bright and Early Books. As with the Beginner Books, he also hired other authors and illustrators to write additional books for the new series. However, he was an absolute perfectionist and required the same exacting standards of the authors who wrote for him that he did of himself.

## A CHILDLIKE QUALITY

In a number of articles later in life, Geisel was asked how he continually produced books that were so captivating to young readers. He often claimed that his work was successful because it was so simplistic in nature. When asked in an interview how he began his books, he replied, "Mine always start with a doodle. I may doodle a couple of animals; if they bite each other, it's going to be a good book. If you doodle enough, the characters begin to take over themselves."[56]

Always pointing out that he refused to grow up, Geisel saw his work as the natural product of a child being given free rein to draw and create. He commented on the fact that he received thousands of drawings from young children each year, and their style was much the same as his—awkward. He claimed that, "I've refined my childish drawing so that it looks professional. But kids exaggerate the same way I do. They overlook things they can't draw, their pencils slip, and they get some funny effects. I've learned to incorporate my pencil slips into my style."[57]

## "PUZZLING MY PUZZLER"

The childlike simplicity of Dr. Seuss's work is belied by the painstaking perfectionism that went into each book he produced. In a number of interviews, Geisel explained that he often experienced writer's block and went through a laborious process to find exactly the right words or colors to say what he meant. He referred to this as "puzzling my puzzler."[58]

Geisel spent countless hours agonizing over one sentence or even one word. He paced his studio floor, flopped himself onto the couch, threw tantrums, and sulked for days on end until he found just what he was looking for. He referred to the enormous mound of discarded drawings and pages of text as the bone pile and claimed that he often wrote five hundred pages for a sixty-page book. "I know my stuff all looks like it was rattled off in

*Dr. Seuss, shown here drawing at his desk, painstakingly searched for exactly the right words to express what he wanted to say in his books.*

twenty-three seconds," he said, "but every word is a struggle and every sentence is like the pangs of birth."[59]

One of the biggest challenges Dr. Seuss faced with his writing was the fact that everything was written in verse. If he couldn't make a particular word work, he had to throw away four entire lines and start over.

## A Colorful Genius

Although Dr. Seuss is most often known for his breakneck rhyme, many of the professionals he worked with regarded his sense of color selection as his true genius. He used color in subtle yet powerful ways. For example, *The 500 Hats of Bartholomew Cubbins* is drawn completely in black and white, except for the candy apple red hat atop the boy's head. This distinction causes the hat and the boy to jump off the page, adding emphasis to Bartholomew's position as the most central and powerful character in the story.

Every art director who worked with Geisel marveled at his unerring ability to select exactly the right color for a given situation. Some claimed, at first, to be frustrated by his refusal to accept a different shade of the color he was looking for. In the end, however, they all learned to defer to his mastery of the infinite color spectrum.

One art director, Grace Clark, recalled a story about a problematic parrot. Dr. Seuss had completed a new book, *Oh Say Can You Say?* and spent hours scrutinizing the Random House printer's color chart for just the right shade of green for a particular parrot. There were sixty different shades of green on the chart and he couldn't find the right one. Failing to explain exactly why none of the colors worked, he simply said they weren't "parroty" enough. In the end, Dr. Seuss had the Random House art department create a whole new shade of green so that his parrot could look exactly the way he had drawn it at home with his colored pencils. Clark would later say, "His color sense is the most sophisticated I've ever run into."[60]

When asked why he went to such great lengths over such minute details, Dr. Seuss often replied that he had a responsibility to put out a streamlined product. Children, he said, "have as much right to quality as their elders."[61] It was this attitude and the books he produced that helped make Dr. Seuss one of the most popular children's authors to date.

# 5 From Politics to Animation

Although Dr. Seuss is known throughout the world as a writer and illustrator of fanciful children's books, few people know of his passionate attitude toward politics and his fervent work in that arena. Geisel was an extremely opinionated person and had no problem sharing his views with anyone who would listen. During the early years of World War II, before America became involved, he felt very strongly that the United States should not ignore the situation in Europe, and worried that the Nazis would eventually become a threat to the United States as well. His involvement in the United States Army took him to Hollywood, where he established himself as a talented writer and animator of war films and documentaries. These experiences helped Geisel throughout the rest of his career, as he would later adapt a number of his famous works for television.

## THE POLITICAL CARTOONIST

Concerned about America's policy of "noninterference" in World War II, Geisel began expressing himself, as he often did, through words and pictures. He first became a regular contributor to a periodical known as *PM* in January 1941. *PM* was a very liberal political newspaper that was, as Geisel put it, "against people who pushed other people around."[62] Representing a philosophy that appeared as an underlying theme in many of his later books, *PM* was a perfect fit for him. He worked for them, off and on, for several years and didn't put out a single book during that time.

The *PM* cartoons were very simply drawn but extremely harsh and cynical. Geisel never sugar-coated any of the messages he was attempting to get across. The targets of his biting sarcasm were usually Nazis, Hitler, Mussolini, Japan, and an organization called America First. America First was an American lobbying group whose members believed that the United States should stay out of the war in Europe. It was also known for having strong racist undertones. In one of his most scathing cartoons for *PM*, Geisel drew an America First member reading a story to a child about "Adolf the Wolf." The caption read, "And the wolf chewed up the children and spit out their bones. . . . But those were foreign children and it really didn't matter."[63]

Very well received at the time, the cartoons received national attention. *News-*

"... and the Wolf chewed up the children and spit out their bones .. But those were <u>Foreign Children</u> and it really didn't matter."

Dr. Seuss ©pm

*Dr. Seuss contributed this cartoon to* PM *magazine before the United States became involved in World War II.*

*week* commented on them and called Geisel's wit "razor-keen."[64] A collection of rarely seen *PM* cartoons was put together in a book released in 1999 called *Dr. Seuss Goes to War*.

Clearly, Geisel had a passion for many social and political issues, and he made a point of standing up for those beliefs from an early age. Many of the themes of his political cartoons, such as oppression of civil rights and an opposition to bigotry,

can be found throughout the pages of the children's books that would occupy the later years of his life.

## HOMETOWN ACTIVISM

In addition to his books, Geisel found a wide variety of outlets for his views on politics—from the local community level up to the White House. Both Ted and his wife Helen were extremely involved in the local community politics of their home in La Jolla, California. As the once-secluded town became a popular tourist destination, Geisel lobbied vehemently against the commercialism he felt threatened to destroy their community. In one case, he lobbied the town council to ban billboard construction in La Jolla. As part of his effort, he wrote and illustrated a pamphlet titled *Signs of Civilization!*, which was a cartoon about two Stone Age businessmen who were locked in competition. Each chiseled out a number of roadside signs to advertise his business until their prehistoric wilderness became a junkyard of billboards and tacky sales gimmicks. The pamphlet ended in vintage Seuss style. It read,

> And, thus between them, with
>     impunity
> They loused up the entire community
>     . . .
> And even the dinosaurs moved away
> From that messed-up spot in the U.S.A.
> Which is why
> Our business men never shall
> Allow such to happen
> in La Jolla, Cal.[65]

## DR. SEUSS GOES TO WAR

Feeling the need to fulfill a larger-scale civic duty and do his part to fight the Nazi menace, Ted Geisel enlisted in the army in December 1942. He was commissioned as a captain and because of his well-known talents was assigned to the Information and Education Division. Stationed in Los Angeles, on the set of the Fox Studios—dubbed Fort Fox—Geisel was responsible for writing and producing war films to help train American troops in everything from international politics to how to survive in the Arctic.

Geisel was in good company. His commanding officer was the well-known Hollywood director Frank Capra, and other members of his unit included Warner Brothers cartoon animators Friz Freleng and Chuck Jones. During his three years

*Hollywood director Frank Capra (pictured) was Dr. Seuss's commanding officer in the army during World War II.*

# THE A-BOMB

*While making films for the United States Army, Geisel often included material that pushed the limits of what was appropriate and acceptable. In "Children's Friend" in the December 17, 1960, issue of the* New Yorker, *E. J. Kahn Jr. retells the story of one film that may have unintentionally gone too far when Dr. Seuss accidentally revealed the government's method of splitting the hydrogen atom to create the first nuclear weapon.*

"Shortly before the first atomic bomb was exploded, Geisel returned to California, where he was ordered to come up with another film for postwar occupation troops—one that would keep them on the alert by reminding them that inattention could lead to a third world war. 'Make that third war a real doozy, Geisel,' he was told. Seeking inspiration, he leafed through the magazine section of a recent Sunday *Times*, where his eye was caught by an article suggesting that there was enough latent energy in a tumbler of water, if man could ever figure out a way of harnessing it, to blow up half the earth. Without further ado, or further research, Geisel knocked out the draft of script suggesting the possibility of unimaginably devastating explosions, and passed it along to his superiors. Two days later, the Pentagon was on the phone, urgently asking where he'd got his facts.

'From the *Times*?' he replied.

'Burn your source of information Geisel,' came the command.

'Burn the *Times*?' he asked.

'Yes, and report by phone as soon as you've carried out your orders,' he was told.

'I had long since thrown away the copy of the paper in question,' Geisel recalls, 'but I wanted to be a good soldier, so I rushed my most reliable sergeant to an out-of-town news dealer, and he bought me a copy of the latest *Times*. We put it in a metal bucket and all marched out into a courtyard and stood in formation and gave the Boy Scout salute while a trusted lieutenant lit a match to it. Then I called Washington and said, "Mission accomplished, sir. We have burned the *Times*." "Well done Geisel," I was told and then they went on with the war.'"

in the army, he and Helen lived in a small apartment in Los Angeles. Ever reliable, Helen helped support them during this time by writing a number of children's books for Disney and Golden Books.

One of the first projects Geisel worked on in the army was a set of illustrations for a pamphlet called *This Is Ann*. It was an informational booklet for the troops on how to avoid malaria, caused by the anopheles mosquito. The pamphlet was later made into a cartoon as one installment in a series of instructional army/navy short films centered around the exploits of a character named Private Snafu. The films focused on a broad range of simple topics and were geared toward the many teenage recruits being brought in to the war effort.

Geisel learned a lot more than just army protocols during his time in the army, however. He gained valuable experience by working with the talented people around him. Most notably, he claimed to have learned about animation from Chuck Jones—despite being ten years his senior—and how to keep his writing short and to the point from Frank Capra.

## WAR FILMS

As his skills and rank increased, Dr. Seuss moved away from simple cartoon shorts and began working on larger projects, the first of which was a film titled *Your Job in Germany*. This live-action film was meant to be an instructional tool for postwar soldiers, explaining what would be expected of them as the United States helped reconstruct Germany after the war ended. It contained very harsh warnings against fraternizing with German citizens—a topic that Geisel had issues with since he was of German descent.

Despite the reservations he had about the film, Geisel spent months traveling back and forth from Washington to Hollywood while researching and writing it. For the narrator, Geisel had interviewed a young actor (who later became president) named Ronald Reagan, but turned him down in favor of someone else.

Once *Your Job in Germany* was complete, Dr. Seuss was assigned the task of taking it to Europe and showing it to a number of generals. This was the only time Geisel approached an actual battlefield, and he recalled owing his life to yet another lucky twist of fate. He took his film reels to a supposedly "quiet" area: Bastogne, Belgium. Shortly after arriving there, he became bored and wandered off to explore. He found himself lost behind German lines and, along with an Allied MP (military police), remained trapped behind enemy lines for three days before being rescued by the British. As it turned out, Geisel's wandering spirit probably saved his life. Just hours after he left Bastogne, the Germans launched an attack on the city. Known as the Battle of the Bulge, it was one of the bloodiest battles in World War II. The base was destroyed, and many of Geisel's fellow officers were killed.

## THE HOLLYWOOD BUG REMAINS

The war ended in 1945, but the Hollywood bug would never leave Dr. Seuss completely. Upon his return to civilian status, he was hired as a staff writer for Warner Brothers Studios. In an effort to capitalize on the American public's enthusiasm for war-related subjects, the studio had taken Geisel's *Your Job in Germany* and remade it into a mainstream documentary. Released under the title *Hitler Lives?* it won an Academy Award for best documentary short subject in 1946. Geisel, however, had problems with his boss at Warner Brothers and didn't remain there very long.

Shortly after, he received a call from the entertainment company RKO asking for his help in rewriting a script of one of his other wartime films: *Know Your Enemy—Japan*. Originally, this had been a twenty-two-minute film similar to the earlier *Your Job in Germany*. Because of some controversy over the film's sympathetic attitude toward the Japanese, however, it was never released. Geisel battled studio executives over creative control issues, and af-

ter thirty-two major revisions, the newly titled *Design for Death* was released into theaters. It was forty-eight minutes long and in 1947 won the Academy Award for best documentary feature.

With a hand in two Oscar-winning films, Dr. Seuss seemed to have a prolific film career ahead of him. However, he felt uncomfortable having to compromise his artistic integrity and answer to the film studio heads. Geisel told a *Life* magazine interviewer, "I found I preferred making my own mistakes rather than being told how to make them, so I went back to writing kids' books."[66]

## ONE MORE TIME

After being back in the book business for about three years, and producing such classics as *If I Ran the Zoo*, *Bartholomew and the Oobleck*, and *McElligot's Pool*, Geisel received a call from an old war buddy, his

*Dr. Seuss traveled to Bastogne, Belgium to promote his military training film,* Your Job in Germany *and narrowly escaped involvement in the Battle of the Bulge (shown here), one of the bloodiest battles of World War II.*

friend P. D. Eastman, who was working for an animation studio called United Productions of America. The studio was interested in producing some unusual films, hoping to offer the public a little variety from the standard mouse-outsmarting-a-cat cartoon. Geisel wrote the script for *Gerald McBoing-Boing*, a story about a boy who could not speak and could communicate only by making strange sounds. Geisel opted not to help illustrate the project because he felt they could find someone better to draw humans. When it was released in 1951, the film did very well and earned yet another Oscar, this time for best cartoon.

## 5,000 FINGERS

Riding on the success of his Hollywood hits, Ted submitted a story idea to Columbia Pictures in 1951. The studio responded with a $35,000 advance to write the script. A live-action film, *The 5,000 Fingers of Dr. T* was a fantasy about a ten-year-old boy who is so bored with his piano lessons that he falls asleep and dreams up an archaic castle where the evil Dr. Terwilliker holds children captive and makes them play the piano in a surreal dungeon sweatshop. The film was very dark and the sets were bizarre.

Geisel was very excited about the project. He saw it as a way to break in to full-

*RKO studios (shown here) hired Dr. Seuss to rewrite the script for the wartime film,* Design for Death. *The movie won an Academy Award for best documentary film in 1947.*

## The 5,000 Hot Dogs of Dr. T

*Geisel considered the movie* The 5,000 Fingers of Dr. T *his greatest professional disaster. An excerpt from the book* Dr. Seuss and Mr. Geisel *by Judith and Neil Morgan describes Geisel and Helen's account of the turmoil on the set.*

"When shooting finally began in March, budget cuts abounded. Helen counted the 'five hundred' boy pianists and found only one hundred and fifty. 'There wasn't enough money to do what should really have been a musical extravaganza,' Kramer [the producer] said later. Helen termed the set a madhouse, 'especially in one scene where [the boys] all have to kick and scream and jump on the piano and drag Dr. T . . . off to the dungeon.'

One of Ted's few happy memories from those months was of the rainy day when the young pianists took a break to gulp down commissary hot dogs; one boy became ill and vomited on his keyboard. 'This started a chain reaction,' Ted recalled, 'causing one after another of the boys to go queasy in the greatest mass upchuck in the history of Hollywood. . . . When the picture was finally released, the critics reacted in much the same manner.'"

length movies. Given a lot of creative control and asked to remain on the set to help out with production, Dr. Seuss and Helen moved up to Los Angeles for the duration of the filming. They wanted to be as close as possible to the production of Geisel's first full-length feature.

Fraught with complications, the film's production was pushed back a number of times. Geisel found that "creative control" was a relative term and he quit the production once, before being coerced back. Severe budget cuts caused the musical numbers to be scaled down, and the number of children in the piano prison was reduced from 500 to 150. Geisel continued to believe in the movie, however, and desperately wanted to be a success in the film

industry. When the film was finally released in 1952, it was a complete disaster. Audiences filed out of the theater after just fifteen minutes, and the critics were not kind. The failure was difficult to take, and Geisel later recalled the film's premiere as "the worst evening of [his] life."[67]

This endeavor cured Geisel of his desire to make movies, and he never again returned to the big screen. However, what he didn't know was that, during the years to come, he would find great success in television adaptations of his books.

## Enter the Small Screen

As the years progressed, Geisel was asked to adapt a number of his books for television.

Always wary of putting out a product that did not meet with his perfectionist standards, he insisted on having an active role in the productions. From 1966 through 1989, Dr. Seuss produced more than ten made-for-television specials for CBS, ABC, and TNT. Several were based on his well-known books such as *The Cat in the Hat* and *The Lorax*, bringing his stories to moving, speaking, and singing life on the small screen.

He also wrote several original screenplays specifically for television. Two of these, *The Grinch Grinches the Cat in the Hat* and *Halloween Is Grinch Night*, won Emmy awards. Although his lesser-known TV credits were the only ones to receive Emmys, some of his better-known works did receive other accolades: *Horton Hears a Who!* earned a Peabody Award, and *The Lorax* received citations from a number of film and TV festivals.

## A HOLIDAY STANDARD

Many of Dr. Seuss's attempts to adapt his books for television were successful. However, one stood out from the rest. In 1971, *How the Grinch Stole Christmas!* entered the living rooms of households all across America. It was a project Dr. Seuss felt very strongly about, and he was extremely concerned that it might not translate well onto television. He was afraid that the songs written for the television version would not do justice to the story's text. Finding the perfect voice for the Grinch was also no easy task. Fortunately, they were able to sign on the talents of

Boris Karloff, the original Hollywood Frankenstein. In the end, Dr. Seuss was thrilled with the adaptation. He was especially pleased with Karloff's rendition of the Grinch, saying, "He [Karloff] took the script and studied it for a week as if it were Shakespeare. He figured out all the nuances. That's one of the reasons why it works so well."[68]

## A GOOD YEAR

The success of the television special was due primarily to the popularity of the book it was adapted from. Published in 1957, the same year as *The Cat in the Hat*, *How the Grinch Stole Christmas!* was an instant classic. According to Clifton Fadiman, a book critic and one of Dr. Seuss's earliest champions, "Grinch is a classic because youngsters today unconsciously prefer the familiar Scrooge motif to be translated into simple, vigorous, jokey language that's truly their own, part of their time and place, appealing to a sense of humor that welcomes the wild, the grotesque, even the mildly lunatic."[69]

As lunatic as it may be, *The Grinch* still incorporates the notion of logical insanity found in most of Dr. Seuss's works. The Whos, for example, are the same creatures found in *Horton Hears a Who!* and are treated with the same continuity as a returning character in any piece of adult literature. A bicycle under the Christmas tree is labeled, "for Jo-Jo," the small boy whose "yop" saved their entire town three years earlier. Many other small details add to the book's sense of reality in an unreal world, such as the carving of "roast beast" instead of roast beef and the refrigerator having a "General Who-Lec-tric" label on it.

In this case, the bridge between fantasy and reality appeared to have crossed over into Dr. Seuss's personal life. There are hidden clues that the Grinch may be a caricature of Dr. Seuss himself. The Grinch says,

> Why, for fifty-three years I've put up
> with it now!
> I MUST stop this Christmas from
> coming! . . . But HOW?[70]

## A VERY CLOSE LOOK AT THE GRINCH

*Many critics attempted to find the deeper meaning and hidden symbolism in Dr. Seuss's books, often dissecting every word and picture. Sometimes Geisel agreed with these analyses and sometimes he claimed that people were reading too much into it. Ruth K. MacDonald offers an in-depth look at* How the Grinch Stole Christmas!, *in her biography* Dr. Seuss.

"In the final picture, where he [the Grinch] is shown carving the roast, his smile is that of the benign [harmless] Cat in the Hat and his hands, before menacing and pointy, no longer seem so devious. That he is seated underneath a wreath at the Who's table nicely rounds out the story pictorially, for the opening page shows a young Who holding the same wreath and looking out at the reader, as though the Who were an illuminated capital from an old manuscript. This same Who with the wreath is shown on the end pages; in fact, the wreath recurs throughout the book as a symbol of the spirit of unity and the attractive festivity of the season. Though the Grinch is not holding the wreath, nor looking through it in the final picture, it emphasizes his change of spirit as it encircles his head like a halo."

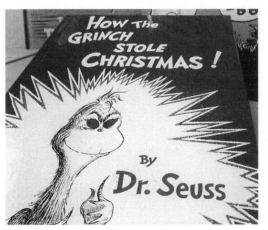

*Some literary critics believe they have uncovered symbolic meaning in* How the Grinch Stole Christmas!

*The Grinch character carved a deep niche in literary mythology.*

Geisel did not like to celebrate Christmas and was exactly fifty-three years old when he wrote this book. Any doubts about the Geisel/Grinch connection would be laid to rest by looking at the back of Dr. Seuss's car, which had vanity plates that read simply, "GRINCH."

Coming out right on the heels of *The Cat in the Hat, How the Grinch Stole Christmas!* helped propel Dr. Seuss into the ranks of the immortals. His publishers launched him on a lengthy parade of public addresses, press conferences, and book signings. In the end, *How the Grinch Stole Christmas!* did more than just succeed. Like the cat with the stovepipe hat, the Grinch became an American institution. The infamous green-furred creature carved a niche for itself not only as a permanent figure in literary mythology but also as a new word in the English language. Similar to the way that Charles Dickens's Scrooge has become synonymous with *miser*, the word *Grinch* is now a noun used to describe someone who doesn't appear to have the Christmas spirit.

Although Geisel never achieved the success in the movie industry that he had hoped for, the success of the Grinch TV special made him a formidable force in animation. Furthermore, Dr. Seuss's experience in filmmaking during World War II helped him gain the necessary skills and make the connections he would need to produce a string of successful animated television specials. Not only were these programs critical and popular successes, but they helped his stories reach an even larger segment of the American public, generation after generation.

# 6 The Message Books

Over the years, people attempted to dissect Dr. Seuss's books in an effort to unravel the hidden mysteries and messages that lie within. Despite these efforts, for most of his career, Geisel claimed never to have written his books with a moral message in mind. "Kids," he said, ". . . can see a moral coming a mile off and they gag at it."[71] However, he did admit once that in every story there is an inherent moral.

## A WISE ELEPHANT

Two of Dr. Seuss's early books—both of which focus on one of his most endearing characters—are continuously identified as containing specific messages about life: *Horton Hatches the Egg* and *Horton Hears a Who!* Horton the elephant is the kind of creature that anyone would want as a friend: He is faithful, kind, and never gives up. In *Horton Hatches the Egg*, he is set with the task of nest-sitting for a lazy bird who would rather be at the beach than care for her offspring. The mother fails to return as promised, but despite inclement weather, despair, harassment by his peers, having his life threatened, and being put on display in a circus freak

*Dr. Seuss often denied including obvious moral messages in his books.*

show, Horton never gives up. The refrain "I meant what I said, and I said what I meant . . . an elephant's faithful one hundred per cent!"[72] rings through the book again and again. In the end, Horton is rewarded for his steadfastness. When the creature hatches from the egg, it turns out to be a tiny elephant with wings, and the book closes with Horton happily returning home with his new child.

Dr. Seuss's second Horton book, *Horton Hears a Who!* seems even more obvious in its message. According to a 1954 review in the *Des Moines Register, Horton Hears a Who!* is "a rhymed lesson in protection of minorities and their rights."[73] In this story, after discovering a voice and then a tiny town on a speck of dust, Horton endeavors to protect it. The other creatures of the forest are unable to hear the Whos' cries for help and decide that Horton is crazy for looking after these insignificant "bugs." They tease him at first, then steal his precious speck, and by the end of the story they have decided to lock him up and boil his friends in Beezle-Nut oil. Horton pleads with them to stop. Again there is one refrain that seems to capture the story's message and recurs throughout the book: "A person's a person, no matter how small!"[74]

When Horton explains to the mayor of Whoville that, although they have the right to exist, it is up to them to make themselves heard, things begin to change. By gathering together and making sure every last Who is doing his part, the tiny society achieves this goal. At last the other animals hear them, and they are saved.

---

## SAVING TRUFFULAS AND MORE

*The Lorax has been used in classrooms and courtrooms across the country to argue for a more healthy attitude toward the environment. "In Pursuit of the Lorax," an article written by Jennifer Zicht in the fall 1991 issue of the* EPA *Journal, talks about the book's value.*

"This book has all the attributes of good literature while serving as an excellent environmental tool. Dr. Seuss's prose is lively, if not zany, clear, and logical. The story rivets the reader's attention, and the message is so amusing and thought-provoking that readers won't put it down.

As an educational tool, *The Lorax* gives readers all the details leading to the tragedy. It shows how an ecosystem functions and how it ultimately disintegrates as a consequence of an individual's selfish actions. It presents both sides of the controversy in an unbiased fashion. Above all, *The Lorax* gives the reader a sense of commitment. As the Lorax retreats from the wasteland, he leaves a stone monument with the word 'unless' etched upon it. The meaning: 'Unless someone like you cares a whole awful lot, nothing is going to get better. It's not.' The tale ends optimistically when the reader is asked to plant the last existing Truffula seed."

Readers and researchers around the world study *Horton Hears a Who!* and other Dr. Seuss stories and wonder whether Geisel wrote the books to make a moral statement or simply to tell a good story. When an interviewer for *U.S. News & World Report* asked that very question, Geisel replied, "Sometimes people find morals where there are none. People have read all kinds of things into *Green Eggs and Ham*, including biblical connotations."[75] Geisel also points out that *Horton Hatches the Egg* came about not from a moral imperative but from the random circumstance of the wind blowing his artwork around the table.

## FASCIST TURTLES AND ANTI-SEMITIC SNEETCHES

Although delivering morals may not have been the primary purpose of Dr. Seuss's early works, his books can be described as vehicles through which he expressed his feelings on a number of issues. By creating and controlling fantastic stories, he could exorcise many of the demons that plagued him. In some cases he was a little more direct in admitting this. In an interview with Jonathan Cott in 1983, for example, Geisel talked about *"Yertle the Turtle* which was modeled on the rise of Hitler."[76] His feelings about fascism, and Nazis in particular, ran deep.

In the same interview he claimed that *"The Sneetches . . .* was inspired by my opposition to anti-semitism."[77] In this book, Dr. Seuss introduced the reader to a race of yellow birdlike creatures that inhabit an unidentified beach. There appear to be two kinds of Sneetches. The ones with stars on their bellies are the upper class, while the plain-bellied Sneetches are outcasts. Dr. Seuss wrote,

> When the Star-Belly Sneetches had
>   frankfurter roasts
> Or picnics or parties or marshmallow
>   toasts,
> They never invited the Plain-Belly
>   Sneetches.
> They left them out cold, in the dark of
>   the beaches.
> They kept them away. Never let them
>   come near.
> And that's how they treated them
>   year after year.[78]

When a stranger arrives on the beach claiming to have a machine that will put stars on their bellies, the plain-bellied Sneetches line up and are instantly transformed into society's upper crust. The other Sneetches are outraged and pay the stranger to remove their stars so that they can remain distinct from the impostors. By the end of the tale, both groups have had their stars added and removed so many times that it is impossible to tell who was who anymore. Ultimately, all the Sneetches come to realize that judging people by their stars—or any other categorical prejudice—is simply pointless.

Even though Dr. Seuss tried to camouflage the messages in his earlier stories, perhaps to not alienate the child reader, it is clear that he had strong feelings on a variety of subjects. Whether the message was thinly veiled or buried deep enough to go unnoticed, there was often a story behind the story. Geisel has been quoted

# A NOT-SO-HIDDEN MESSAGE

*In her biographical work* Dr. Seuss, *Ruth K. MacDonald discusses the powerful messages found in Geisel's later books.*

"His purpose in each of those [later] books has been to challenge readers of all ages, including younger ones, to action, in order to resolve dire threats to life as we know it. His confrontation of the issue of nuclear war in *The Butter Battle Book* is the most shocking, since it confronts universal death, an issue that offends the sensibilities of most adults so deeply that it is commonly thought an inappropriate issue to present to children. But as in *The Lorax*, Dr. Seuss does not ask simply that children contemplate the issue, thereby torturing themselves with unthinkable thoughts. He calls for action and enables the child reader to do something. In *The Lorax*, children are taught about the frivolity of some consumer goods and the . . . harm of buying those goods if their manufacture damages the ecosystem. As part of the solution, children are given the option of cultivating living things and protecting them so that they can flourish. In *The Butter Battle Book*, the argument between the Yooks and the Zooks is so extreme that most children can be led to see that discussion, negotiation, and peaceful coexistence are all options, and that even uncomfortable coexistence is preferable to mutually assured self-destruction. Dr. Seuss is not simply trying to make children aware of these important issues; he is also [suggesting] models for children to follow. He wants to empower children, rather than drive them to despair. He also implies that children are smart enough to understand these issues; they need not be helpless victims. In fact, empowering children and encouraging mastery and independence is one of the central themes in all Dr. Seuss's works for children."

as saying that many of his books "come from . . . the part of my soul that started out to be a teacher."[79]

In his later years, Dr. Seuss seemed less concerned with hiding his messages. A number of his books from the 1970s and '80s were blatant statements on issues that affected not only him but the world.

After the death of his first wife, Helen, in 1967, Geisel seemed to become concerned with weightier issues. Over the years he sat in his studio and watched with increasing dismay as condominiums and look-alike houses filled in the landscape. He was extremely concerned about the overdevelopment of natural habitats and became angry that people were abusing the environment with such reckless abandon.

Because so much of what he read on conservation was boring and preachy, Geisel decided to write a story about ecology that was entertaining enough to appeal to children yet poignant enough to get a real message across. He struggled for months on the project and got nowhere. Finally, his new wife, Audrey, suggested that they take a trip to Africa to get Geisel's mind off his work.

After several days of relaxing, the couple was sitting by a pool at a resort in Kenya when Dr. Seuss's writer's block vanished. "About a mile away," he said, "a herd of elephants came over a hill. I don't know what happened. I grabbed a laundry list that I had beside me and wrote the whole book in 45 minutes. I've looked at elephants ever since but it has never happened again."[80] Less than one year later, *The Lorax* appeared on bookshelves across America.

## "UNLESS . . ."

As with most Dr. Seuss characters, the Lorax is difficult to categorize. He is described

*Dr. Seuss addressed environmental issues in* The Lorax *while taking notice of the overdevelopment in his hometown of La Jolla, California (pictured).*

as sort of a man. Short, furry, and emerging from a tree stump, he appears to be some kind of nature spirit. Dr. Seuss claimed that *The Lorax*, a tale of greed and shortsightedness, was his favorite piece of work.

The book tells the story of the Once-ler, a clothing manufacturer who arrives in a pristine forest and begins to chop down the unusual Truffula trees in order to harvest raw materials. The Once-ler is making something called Thneeds, which are nondescript articles of clothing that, according to him, everyone needs. The Lorax pesters him throughout the book and warns him of the damage he is causing. Refusing to heed the creature's advice, the Once-ler proceeds to destroy the entire forest, causing all of its inhabitants to abandon their homes and wander off in search of refuge. Ultimately ashamed of what he has done, the Once-ler locks himself up in the tower of his abandoned factory. Many years later, a small boy shows up in the dead forest and the industrialist-turned-hermit tells him the tragic tale of how the once-beautiful forest was laid to waste. As the story closes, the Once-ler yells down from his tower to the boy,

> Now that *you're* here,
> the word of the Lorax seems perfectly
>     clear.
> UNLESS someone like you cares a
>     whole awful lot,
> nothing is going to get better.
> It's not.[81]

He then tosses down the last Truffula seed and charges the boy with planting it, caring for it, and rebuilding the forest.

## A LEARNING TOOL

When it first came out in 1971, *The Lorax* was not one of Dr. Seuss's biggest hits. Many people found it to be a very dark and heavy departure from his earlier works. However, nearly a decade later, when the environmental movement kicked in to full swing in the United States, the book saw a huge increase in sales. It was suddenly touted as one of the best books ever written on the subject of conservation.

Articles about its usefulness in introducing young people to the concept of environmental protection continue today. One article labeled it "one of the most poignant and sobering pieces of environmental literature written for a six-year-old."[82] Today, of course, there are a large number of conservation-themed books geared toward young children. It has become an almost trendy topic. Dr. Seuss, however, was a pioneer, addressing the subject back in 1971 not as a gimmick but as an expression of his own personal dissatisfaction with people's treatment of the earth.

*The Lorax* doesn't just paint a picture of doom and gloom, scaring children into submission. It offers several constructive suggestions for effecting change. It encourages people to speak out loudly against those who pollute the earth and to be informed consumers, never making purchases that unduly harm natural habitats. Perhaps the most powerful message comes at the end when Dr. Seuss reminds children of their own importance. Having the story close with the young boy planting the last Truffula seed conveys the no-

*Some members of the logging industry see* The Lorax *as an attack on their livelihood.*

tion that all it takes to begin healing the environment is one small first step—something any child can do.

## A Controversial Book?

Most people who read *The Lorax* see it as a wonderful and important tale. Some, however, do not appreciate its message. The book has been at the center of controversy a number of times. Some members of the logging and paper mill industry, for example, see it as an attack on their livelihood. In one case, the controversy came to a head in a school board showdown.

In the fall of 1989, a second grader came home to his father—who worked in the logging industry of northern California—and asked why he was destroying the forest. The boy went on to explain that his class had just read *The Lorax* and he felt that his father was making a living by taking homes away from all the creatures of

the forest. Outraged, the man organized other members of the local logging community in an effort to have the book banned from schools. He rallied a lot of support, and the group took out an ad in the local paper, claiming that "our kids are being brainwashed. We've got to stop this crap right now!"[83]

The situation culminated in a heated debate at an open meeting of the local school board. Pro-*Lorax* and pro-loggers argued their cases and, ultimately, the board decided to keep *The Lorax* on the shelves. When adapting the story for television, though, the anti-industrialist overtones were scaled down at the request of CBS, who feared they might have a difficult time getting commercial sponsors for the program.

Geisel responded to complaints about his book by saying, "[*The Lorax*] is about people who raise hell in the environment and leave nothing behind."[84] He claimed that the book is not a direct attack against

*His only book for adults since* The Seven Lady Godivas, You're Only Old Once! *came under much scrutiny. Although it sold as well as any other Dr. Seuss book, the critics were split on their opinions of it. In an excerpt from the biography* Dr. Seuss, *Ruth K. MacDonald talks about the book's purpose.*

"The book's date of publication was 2 March 1986, Dr. Seuss's eighty-second birthday. It is dedicated to the remaining classmates of Dr. Seuss's from the class of 1925 at Dartmouth. These reminders of the author's age, and the book's title, prepare the reader for an investigation into the issues surrounding old age, especially the way that the medical profession deals with old people's physical complaints. Though lighthearted and comical, the book's main point is a critique of the medical profession and the costly, irrelevant, rude, and sometimes pointless treatments given to patients. The book takes potshots at medical specialties, tests, prescriptions, and billing procedures, all of which the author had recently submitted to during a bout of serious illness. It satirizes nearly everything that happens to a patient once he submits himself and his pocketbook to the medical profession."

specific U.S. industries but about his frustration over the *irresponsible* waste of natural resources. Although the Lorax was unable to save his forest from the ravages of the Once-ler, his story lives on to help prevent the same from happening to other forests the world over.

## YET ANOTHER BATTLE

Although *The Lorax* saw its share of media attention over the years, none of Dr. Seuss's books caused quite as much controversy as *The Butter Battle Book*. Released in 1984, this book was clearly an allegory about the dangers of nuclear warfare. The story is about two groups of people, the Yooks and the Zooks, who have a mutual hatred and distrust of each other based on nothing more than a difference of opinion over which side bread should be buttered on. There are armed border patrols who maintain a strict separation between the two communities. When one side upgrades its weaponry from a simple stick to a slingshot, the other side responds by creating an enormous triple slingshot. The arms race escalates until eventually both sides are standing at the border holding a small buzzing pellet that has the capacity to blow up the entire countryside. The Yook border guard's young grandson looks on in fear as the book ends in a standoff.

*The Butter Battle Book* did quite well, breaking a record at the time by being the only piece of children's literature to appear on the *New York Times'* adult best-seller list for six months. The story is full of classic Dr. Seuss rhyme and rhythm, but some parents and critics felt the subject matter was simply too frightening for a child.

Some people also felt that it trivialized the arms race. One journalist, John Garvey, said that *The Butter Battle Book* distorts the truth by reducing very real conflicts to something as silly as which side you butter your bread on. He claimed that there are real issues in the world, such as nations that quell people's civil rights and commit horrible atrocities. Preventing those countries from overstepping their bounds requires a powerful military presence.

The biggest problem, however, concerned the ending. Most children's authors agree that one of the elements of a good children's book is a clear, concise ending. Children don't like to end a story with anything unresolved. Normally, even Dr. Seuss agreed with that philosophy. He was quoted once as saying, "A child identifies with the hero, and it is a personal tragedy to him when things don't come out all right."[85]

In the case of *The Butter Battle Book*, however, it appears that he used that notion in reverse. He intentionally left the ending hanging in the balance, perhaps to drive home the message that the arms race and nuclear warfare are unresolved issues. The book was borne out of Dr. Seuss's anger over the situation that adults have left the world in. One critic, Ruth MacDonald, points out that the last page may sum up Dr. Seuss's feeling on the matter: The young boy is perched in a tree watching the stalemate. MacDonald

*Dr. Seuss signs a copy of* The Butter Battle Book, *which took on the weighty issue of the arms race.*

believes this shows that the actions of the grandfather—representing the adults of the world—are putting the grandson—representing the children of the world—in great danger.

Over the years, many children have written to Dr. Seuss suggesting endings for the book. Some side with the Yooks, since the story is told from their perspective, but the overwhelming majority suggest that both sides need to sit down and talk it out.

An article in *Young Children* magazine suggests using the book as a tool in the classroom. By having children role-play the situation and engage in a discussion of the Yook and Zook points of view, teachers can help students learn the concepts of tolerance and negotiation. This, the article points out, is the real message of the book.

Dr. Seuss did admit that the book is not exclusively for children. However, he claimed, it deals with a topic that, although frightening, is a reality of the world children are growing up in and one that is important for them to know about and understand.

## YOU'RE ONLY OLD ONCE!

Toward the end of his life, Geisel experienced a long series of medical challenges. He battled everything from cancer to cataracts. At one point, his eyes were so bad that he was in danger of losing his

### A LITTLE LIME GOES A LONG WAY

*Despite his age and failing health, Geisel maintained his sense of humor and quirkiness in his later years. Shortly after his death, Cathy Goldsmith, who worked with Geisel on his final book* Oh, the Places You'll Go! *discussed an unusual gift he gave her in an article for* Publisher's Weekly.

"This sense of the unexpected extended into [Geisel's] personal relationships as well. In June 1989, I had just returned from California where I had been working with Ted on *Oh, the Places You'll Go!* While there, I was quite taken with a dwarf lime tree growing in the garden outside the house. A few days later, a package arrived, looking for all the world like a black-velvet jeweler's box. That's exactly what it was, but there wasn't any jewelry inside. There was one perfect little lime. The note said that as recognition for all my help, I'd been voted a one-third share in the Meyer Lime Tree. (Ted and the Cat in the Hat held the other two shares.) That one lovely lime was my share of that year's crop. At the time, I thought it was a very special gift. It doesn't begin to compare, however, to the many wondrous books that Ted gave to all of us during his lifetime."

*Dr. Seuss, shown here in his La Jolla office, wrote the adult book,* You're Only Old Once! *because he was frustrated with physicians' lack of respect to the elderly.*

sight. During the travails of his later years he became increasingly frustrated with the medical profession. He was quick to point out the doctors who were kind and treated him well—in fact, he even dedicated a book to his eye doctor—but he felt that, in general, the elderly were treated with little respect by the majority of doctors. The result of these frustrations was yet another book. At the age of eighty-two, Dr. Seuss published *You're Only Old Once!*

## WRITING FOR ADULTS?

The book garnered mixed reviews. Many people found it an amusing, if cantankerous, look at the medical industry. Others felt that it was not up to the same standards as his other works. The *New York Times Book Review* said, "There's something amiss in the blithe assumption that the sort of rhymes which delight a four-year-old . . . will still entertain when read alone through bifocals."[86] However, the book sold very well and spent many weeks on the adult best-seller list.

*You're Only Old Once!* made no attempt to masquerade as a piece of children's literature. It was written primarily for adults and is even subtitled "A Book for Obsolete Children" (the term Dr. Seuss had always used when talking about adults). The back dust jacket further warns consumers:

> Is this a children's book?
> Well . . . not immediately.
> You buy a copy for your child now
> and you give it to him on his 70th
> birthday.[87]

In an interview right after its release, Geisel talked about the many frustrating hours he spent in doctors' offices waiting for his next unpleasant test or bit of news. He said, "I began to take sketch pads with me and amuse myself by thinking of the horrible things they were going to do to me next."[88] A short time later, perhaps as a kind of therapy, he completed his Seussian account of what he had been through.

## THE GRAND FINALE

Most people, by the age of eighty-five, are long-since retired and have grown accustomed to a slower pace of life. Dr. Seuss was no ordinary person. He was still in his studio from 10:00 A.M. until 6:00 P.M. each day, drawing, writing, and working. He had begun work on a book about lawyers but found that he hated them so much that the book was coming out very angry. After abandoning work on that project and another book about religion, he began to put together what would be his last book. *Oh, the Places You'll Go!* was released in 1990 and was an instant success.

Bigger than anything he had done since *The Cat in the Hat, Oh, the Places You'll Go!* spent more than two years on the *New York Times* adult best-seller list and sold more than 1.5 million copies in that time. Ten years after its first publication, it still manages to make a return to many best-seller lists each May and June, when thousands of people buy it as a gift for graduating high school and college students.

A simple story with a very profound message, *Oh, the Places You'll Go!* is about a young boy who goes out and faces the challenges the world has in store for him. In an interview with *Life* magazine, Geisel said, "The theme is limitless horizons and hope. I am concerned that children today do not think beyond their problems."[89]

Considered by some to be the culmination of his life's work, *Oh, the Places You'll Go!* maintained the classic Dr. Seuss style of a colorful rhyming tale meant to entertain children. This simple, amusing, and poignant story, however, has managed to speak to millions of people across all racial, age, and gender lines about the power they have over their own lives. Dr. Seuss was never afraid to live his life, and the messages he spent so many years playfully delivering to the world have, in his absence, managed to take on a life of their own.

# Chapter

# 7 The Immortal Dr. Seuss

Artist Andy Warhol once said that all people receive fifteen minutes of fame during their lifetime. Some people achieve great things and manage to stretch that out to months or even years. Dr. Seuss was one of those rare individuals who was talented and fortunate enough to enjoy a kind of fame that endured throughout most of his adult life. For more than sixty years, Ted Geisel was known and respected, in a variety of mediums, as a creative genius who managed to repeatedly reinvent both himself and the field he worked in.

## A REAL DOCTOR?

As early as 1955, even before *The Cat in the Hat*, Dr. Seuss's talents were so well-respected that he was invited to his alma mater for a very special honor. On the thirtieth anniversary of his graduation from Dartmouth, Theodor Geisel was granted an honorary doctorate degree. University president John Sloan Dickey delivered an impassioned speech at the ceremony. His words summed up why Geisel was being granted such an honor and expressed what many of Dr. Seuss's fans had always felt

about him. Dickey said, "As author and artist you single-handedly have stood . . . between a generation of exhausted parents and the demon dragon of unexhausted children on a rainy day. . . . As always with the best of humor, behind the fun there has been intelligence, kindness, and a feel for humankind."[90] Always seeing the humor

*Dartmouth University president, John Sloan Dickey (pictured), gave an impassioned speech at the ceremony honoring Theodor Seuss Geisel with an honorary doctorate degree.*

in life, Dr. Seuss joked about his new title: Dr. Dr. Seuss.

As the years passed, Geisel gained more popularity and won more critical acclaim for his work. Invitations from universities came on a regular basis. In total, he received eight honorary doctorates throughout his life from institutions such as Princeton, Brown, and the University of Hartford (Connecticut).

In June 1977, Dr. Seuss attended one such ceremony to receive his third Ph.D. at Lake Forest College, just outside Chicago. Upon his arrival, he was surprised to find out that he was also expected to deliver the graduating class's commencement address. In a rushed frenzy, he scribbled notes on scraps of paper as officials drove him to the ceremony. With his usual discomfort at public appearances, he stood up, fumbled for his notes, and proceeded to deliver a seventy-five-second speech titled "My Uncle Terwilliger on the Art of Eating Popovers."

My uncle ordered popovers
From the restaurant's bill of fare.
And when they were served,
He regarded them
With a penetrating stare . . .
Then he spoke great Words of
    Wisdom
As he sat there on that chair:
"To eat these things,"
said my uncle,
"you must exercise great care.
You may swallow down what's
    solid . . .
BUT . . .
You *must* spit out the air!"

## AN UNEXPECTED BOOK SIGNING

*Judith and Neil Morgan retell a story of one of Dr. Seuss's very last impromptu public appearances toward the end of his life in their book* Dr. Seuss and Mr. Geisel.

"In May friends persuaded Ted and Audrey to come to La Valencia [one of their favorite restaurants] for dinner with his old co-conspirator [journalist] Art Buchwald. Painfully aware of his worsening jaw condition, Ted repeatedly asked if Buchwald could understand him. It had been months since he had felt able to appear at his favorite restaurant, and being there perked him up. Buchwald slipped across [the street] to a bookstore, where he scrawled a sign and hung it in the window: DR. SEUSS IS HAVING DINNER ACROSS THE STREET. Soon chefs, waiters and strangers formed a respectful [line], waiting to approach Ted, one or two at a time, with books for autographing. He signed cheerfully, and every Dr. Seuss book in that store in English, Spanish or French was sold."

And . . .
As *you* partake of the world's bill
   of fare,
That's darned good advice to follow.
Do a lot of spitting out the hot air.
And be careful what you swallow.[91]

When he was finished, there was chaos in the audience. Students cheered, threw their caps in the air, and went wild with delight. Geisel was overwhelmed. This was his first experience with a generation of young adults who had been raised to view him as nothing less than a genius and a celebrity. The adulation continued throughout the remainder of his life, and he was asked to speak at an endless list of college graduation ceremonies, obliging when he could, and using the "Uncle Terwilliger" speech over and over.

At one appearance, his status of pop culture hero was never more evident or appreciated. In 1985, he was scheduled to attend Princeton University's commencement ceremony, as a keynote speaker and to receive another honorary doctorate. Geisel was extremely sick that year and had spent months in and out of hospitals and doctors' offices. Still, he resolved to attend the ceremony. As he stepped up to the podium to address the audience, the entire graduating class stood up and shouted in unison, "I am Sam! Sam I am!"[92] and proceeded to recite the entire text of *Green Eggs and Ham.* Stunned, Geisel forgot his pain and rambled through Uncle Terwilliger's trusty words of wisdom. Inspired and energized by this rally of support, he went home and completed work on *You're Only Old Once!*

## THE BALLOON EXPANDS

In 1984, Geisel received what was probably his greatest honor. He was awarded a special Pulitzer Prize–citation. According to the judging committee, the citation was "for his contribution over nearly half a century to the education and enjoyment of America's children and their parents."[93] The award catapulted him, once again, into the limelight. Geisel was hounded by television and newspaper reporters from all over the world. His face was plastered on countless magazines and was suddenly as recognizable as the fanciful characters he had spent a lifetime creating. This new attention even led to a dinner at the White House, where Dr. Seuss reminisced with President Ronald Reagan about having turned him down for the role of narrator in the war film *Your Job in Germany.*

The public demand for everything Seuss continued. In 1985, a friend approached Geisel about creating a museum exhibit at the San Diego Museum of Art based on a retrospective of his life. At first, Dr. Seuss was skeptical about the project, claiming that there wouldn't be enough material. After a thorough search of Dr. Seuss's personal and professional archives, however—not to mention the walls of his home—the two found more than enough material.

The exhibit opened on May 17, 1986. The Museum of Art building was adorned with a twenty-two-foot plywood Cat in the Hat looking down from the roof. Geisel joked that "[The museum officials] had tried everything for years to keep the pigeons off their roof. Rubber snakes,

*A twenty-two-foot* Cat In The Hat *character above the Modern Art building in San Diego, California where Dr. Seuss's works went on display in 1986.*

owls, spikes, chemicals . . . the first thing that worked was the Cat in the Hat!"[94]

Inside, the exhibit was decorated with banners and graphics. It contained a total of 252 drawings, illustrations, manuscripts, paintings, and original book proofs. There were examples of his early work from the *Jack-O'-Lantern, PM*, and *Judge*. There were even Flit ads and a number of original pieces of art. The exhibit remained at the San Diego Museum of Art for ten weeks and was visited by nearly a quarter of a million people. This set new attendance records for the museum, and the gift shop was hard-pressed to keep the shelves stacked with copies of his books.

The event was such a huge success that the organizers decided to take it on the road. Over a period of two years, it traveled to a number of U.S. cities, often accompanied by Dr. Seuss and his wife, Audrey. At the end of the tour, the materials found a permanent home in the "Geisel Room" of the University of California at San Diego's special collections library.

## ALL GOOD THINGS . . .

In 1960, while E. J. Kahn Jr. was researching the first extensive biographical article on Dr. Seuss, he interviewed many people about their opinions of the man and his work. One seven-year-old boy named Tony had a very sobering response: "When Dr. Seuss dies, that's going to be some awful day."[95]

On September 24, 1991, at the age of eighty-seven, Theodor Seuss Geisel passed away. He had lived a long and extraordinary life. He filled the world with a kind of fun and reckless abandon that had never been seen before, and he lived out all of his dreams. Somehow, though, his death still felt unfair. The headlines of every newspaper in the nation and many around the world announced the sad news on September 25. A banner headline across the front page of the *New York Times* read, "DR. SEUSS, MODERN MOTHER GOOSE, DIES AT 87."[96]

One columnist, Ellen Goodman, disliked the Mother Goose comparison, reminding people that Dr. Seuss stood apart from other children's authors by being—in his own words—"subversive as Hell."[97] She wrote, "[He would] side with the young and dismiss the rest of us for what we are, 'obsolete children.' . . . In Dr. Seuss' reading room, it is still possible to laugh and think at the same time."[98] Several cartoonists drew homages to him, including one in which the Grinch, disguised as the grim reaper, came to collect Dr. Seuss.

An article in that week's *Time* magazine proclaimed that Dr. Seuss "was one of the last doctors to make house calls—some 200 million of them in 20 languages." The article went on to discuss his many achievements, and ended with a very appropriate summation: "It was T. S. Geisel who provoked all the chortles [laughs], but it's old Dr. Seuss who has joined the immortals."[99]

## WRITING FROM THE GREAT BEYOND

At the time of his death, his final work, *Oh, the Places You'll Go!* had been on the *New York Times'* best-seller list for a year and a half. It would remain there for quite some time, but that was not the end of his publishing career. Since his death, several of his unpublished works have been released. In 1995, *Daisy-Head Mayzie,* his only book with a female protagonist, landed on the shelves. That same year a book of his abstract art titled *The Secret Art of Dr. Seuss* came out. In the spirit of the wave of pop psychology books that flew off bookstore shelves in the '90s, Random House released *Seussisms: Wise and Witty Prescriptions for Living from the Good Doctor* in 1997, a tiny volume of quotes from various Dr. Seuss books. Even his political cartoons of the 1930s and '40s have been repackaged and put out in a book called *Dr. Seuss Goes to War.*

## A PERMANENT FIXTURE

Geisel's status of pop culture hero, which really took off in the early 1970s, has lived on beyond the man himself. Dr. Seuss became not just a prolific author but a piece of Americana. References to his work are a routine part of the country's culture. In 1981, New York City mayor Ed Koch was embroiled in a very public battle against the city council president Carol Bellamy. During one of their press meetings, Bellamy presented Koch with a copy of *Yertle the Turtle*, saying, "Some days Ed Koch wakes up in the morning and decides he wants to be Yertle for the day. Whenever that happens, I find myself with a terrible case of indigestion."[100]

In 1984, New York governor Mario Cuomo made a public statement encouraging people to read *The Butter Battle Book*, claiming that it was a magnificent book that would help children gain a clearer understanding of nuclear war issues. Dr. Seuss was even referenced on one of the biggest pop culture hits of the late twenti-

*Wartime cartoons by Dr. Seuss (like the one pictured) have been collected in a book called* Dr. Seuss Goes to War.

# A Cause to Celbrate

*Whenever Ted finished a book, he flew to New York and read it in person to the executives at Random House. In "Children's Friend," an article for the* New Yorker *in 1960, E. J. Kahn describes what happened when Dr. Seuss arrived with a new book.*

"When Random House hears that Geisel is on the way with another pot of gold, excitement runs high, and when he arrives, all hands convene in the office of Louise Bonino, the juvenile editor, for a reading and showing of the latest Dr. Seuss. Even the switchboard operators have been known to leave their post, to the consternation of television producers, lecture agents, Nobel prize winners, and other outsiders vainly seeking the ear of [publisher] Bennett Cerf. Geisel, always a high-strung man, is at his tensest during these performances. At the close of one of them, he retreated in dejection to the Madison Hotel, where he usually stays while in New York, and spent a week rewriting three pages, because he felt that nobody at Random House had laughed hard enough at them. Many authors who have turned in a manuscript and learned that it has been accepted are happy to leave the technicalities of its transformation into a book up to their publishers. Not Geisel. Invading the production department, he will dump three or four moldy bits of crayon, or some scraps torn from matchbooks, onto [the art designer's] desk and say that they are precisely the shades of color he wants used in this or that illustration. That it is often extremely difficult to match up printing ink with crayon does not bother him. Random House has learned to ride with his punches. 'From a genius you tolerate a little bit more,' one editor there has observed."

eth century: On one episode of *The Simpsons*, Lisa Simpson referred to *Yertle the Turtle* as possibly the best book ever written on the subject of turtle stacking.

Geisel's fan base seems only to have increased with time. Today, for example, there are several sanctioned Dr. Seuss clubs at universities across the nation. Students in these organizations gather on a regular basis to celebrate the writings of a man they consider to have been a strong influence on their formative years.

Dr. Seuss's works are also cited in a number of college classes. Bowling Green University in Ohio, for example, has a course on popular culture in which the appeal of *How the Grinch Stole Christmas!* is discussed. The professor, Jack Nachbar, explains part of the appeal, saying, "Whoville is like a nice little commune [that delivers] an anti-materialism message."[101]

Furthermore, although Ted Geisel never owned a computer during his life, Dr. Seuss has recently become a permanent fixture in cyberspace. There are countless websites devoted to the man and his works. While surfing these sites, visitors can learn about Geisel's life, read some of his works, download graphics of his illustrations, play games based on his characters, and even chat with other Dr. Seuss enthusiasts.

## Springfield or Seussville?

In addition to these accolades, Geisel's hometown of Springfield, Massachusetts, has always been extremely proud of its most famous resident. To celebrate his life, the town plans to erect a wonderful collection of Seuss-inspired statues. The local Springfield council decided to build a $4 million memorial to Dr. Seuss.

The memorial will consist of six statues, each representing a part of Dr. Seuss's legacy. The sculptures will be created by Lark Grey Dimond-Cates, Geisel's stepdaughter from his second marriage. Included in the walk-through display will be a six-foot Cat in the Hat and a sixteen-foot stack of turtles, with Yertle perched at the top. There will also be a large open book, standing upright and surrounded by Seuss characters peeking around the sides. In the open pages of the book will be a chair, just the right size for sitting and reading.

The collection's center piece will have a place of honor in front of the very library where Geisel spent so many hours of his youth, gaining the love of reading that would fuel his creative endeavors for the rest of his life. It will be a statue of Geisel working at his desk with the Cat in the Hat looking over his shoulder. "It's like a double portrait," according to Dimond-Cates. "It has to be perfect. Not just for my reputation—it's my family."[102]

## Stage and Screen

Fans don't have to go to Springfield, however, to be reminded of Dr. Seuss's legacy. When he died, he was in negotiations to produce a film version of *Oh, the Places You'll Go!* That project is still in negotiation, but several other projects have come to fruition.

A full-length live-action version of *How the Grinch Stole Christmas!* will be released into theaters in November 2000. Starring Jim Carrey as the Grinch, the Universal Pictures film has been the subject of an enormous publicity campaign. This big-budget feature will be both a wonderful piece of nostalgia for two generations of obsolete children and a perfect high-tech introduction to the holiday classic for the next generation. Universal also has the rights to a similar production of *The Cat in the Hat.* Presumably, if the first movie does well at the box office, the second won't be far behind.

Dr. Seuss will even be in the theater in the new millennium. A full-scale Broadway musical was scheduled to open in

New York toward the end of 2000. Titled *The Seussical*, it will be a montage of Dr. Seuss's books and characters brought to life and set to music and dance. The show received positive feedback during its cross-country tour and should provide theatergoers with a whole new way of looking at Whos and Sneetches.

*Jim Carrey will star in the full-length, live-action version of* How the Grinch Stole Christmas!

## THE LESSONS CONTINUE

Although entertainment was a large part of Dr. Seuss's appeal, there was always more to his nonsense than mere nonsense. Geisel always wanted to be a teacher. With the advent of his Beginner Books, he managed to do just that. His books helped hundreds of thousands of young people learn that reading can be fun. Fortunately, the lessons he shared with the world did not die with him. Today, not only are his books still used in classrooms and homes around the world, but they continue to grow and evolve.

One of the most innovative and critically acclaimed recent adaptations of his work involves interactive CD-ROM programs. Both *Green Eggs and Ham* and *Dr. Seuss's ABC* have been adapted as part of a series of educational materials called Living Books. These programs allow young children to explore the text and illustrations of the book in an interactive manner. They can match words with images, read along with the program, or play a variety of games linked to the book. Both of these programs have received sterling reviews in educational computing circles.

On the Internet, one can find websites that contain Seuss-inspired lesson plans. A number of teachers around the country have developed class lessons based on the works of Dr. Seuss. The lessons range from simple reading exercises to involved role-playing activities geared toward heightening social awareness. Many teachers have posted their ideas on the World Wide Web in an effort to share the activities with as many colleagues as possible.

In addition, a recent issue of *International Wildlife* magazine had a short spread extolling the virtues of *The Lorax* as an instrument of public awareness about conserving the environment. And the television version of *The Butter Battle Book* was broadcast in the former Soviet Union on New Year's Day 1990 in the hopes of sending a message about the fruitlessness of nuclear armament. When the Soviet Union fell apart and its newly independent satellite nations began warring over borders, Dr. Seuss's works were again called into service through a joint effort between Random House and NATO (the North Atlantic Treaty Organization): *The Sneetches* was translated into Serbo-Croation and distributed to chil-

---

## TO BUILD AN ISLAND

*In 1999, Universal Studios opened a new theme park in Orlando, Florida, called Islands of Adventure. One of the five islands, Seuss Landing, was designed as a living re-creation of Dr. Seuss's most famous stories. An article in* Amusement Business Magazine *describes some of the story behind its creation.*

"To help achieve the goal of being true to Seussean architecture, the building facades were all carved out of foam. The repeating Seussean icons of stairways, arches and stripes are carried throughout the area. In addition to the challenges of building with no right angles, the Seussean color requirements also created a challenge. 'Developing the palette was an on-going process,' [added show producer Lisa Girolami.] 'There are 500 different colors here, some off-the-shelf, most custom created. That number sounds excessive, but it was needed because we were true to the books, and color was an important element in bringing those images off the pages and into 3-D for the first time.' In addition to the challenges of architecture, how to landscape the whimsical world also posed a challenge. The knowledge and hard work of landscape architect Patrice Ragusa was the answer. [Girolami states,] 'She [Ragusa] worked hard at making sure that not only the trees and bushes fit in, but that the color of any flower would complement everything else.' She [Girolami] pointed out a flowering tree, whose blossoms blended into the background colors of the carousel. Along Mulberry Street, one of the Mulberry trees is from Mulberry, Fla., and most of the sculpted trees and topiary were purchased from one private collection."

dren in Eastern Europe in an effort to introduce the notion of tolerance.

An article in the November 22, 1999 issue of *Newsweek* even claimed that the good doctor's books can help treat dyslexia. When discussing useful tools to help dyslexics overcome their handicap, the article suggests "just about anything by Dr. Seuss, because of the rhyming and wordplay in the texts. . . . Research consistently shows that kids who are exposed to rhymes are more likely to hear the individual sounds of language."[103]

## The Dr. Seuss Foundation

After Geisel's death, his widow established the Dr. Seuss Foundation. Audrey Geisel wanted to make sure that her husband's message would continue to reach children and help them learn to read. The foundation is designed to encourage children to begin reading for pleasure at an early age and works with private corporations, educational groups, and philanthropic organizations to bring Dr. Seuss books and other materials to the underprivileged.

In 1993, the Kellogg Corporation, in conjunction with the Dr. Seuss Foundation, donated more than 500,000 Dr. Seuss books to nearly two thousand schools that serve disadvantaged youths in an effort to help fight the battle against illiteracy. Each year the foundation donates money to scholarships, various charities, and zoos. Today, a portion of the sales of all Dr. Seuss books goes to the foundation.

Each year on his birthday, Dr. Seuss received thousands of cards and letters. Perhaps his best birthday present, however, came seven years after he had passed away. In 1998, a New Jersey schoolteacher by the name of Sharon Suskin was desperately trying to come up with an innovative way to get her kids to read. With the help of some colleagues, she created a program called Read Across America. On March 2, in honor of Dr. Seuss's birthday, teachers, parents, and librarians were encouraged to sit down and read a story to a child. The program, endorsed by the National Education Association (NEA) and also dubbed Cat in the Hat Day, is supposed to send the message that reading can be fun, rather than just a chore. The program's coordinator, David McGloin, felt that "It's a way to get adults to sit down with children for a while. It's a way of sharing the value of reading and community."[104]

The event was such a success in 1998 that the NEA now promotes it as an annual event both to honor the memory of Dr. Seuss and to help bring national attention to the problem of illiteracy. Libraries and schools host Dr. Seuss plays and read-alongs for the day. Audrey Geisel has even read her favorite Dr. Seuss stories at the San Diego Public Library. In 1999, 20 million children took part in the event, and in 2000 the day was launched with the Cat in the Hat ringing the bell to open the New York Stock Exchange.

## Own a Piece of Seuss

After her husband's death, Audrey's lawyers warned her of the danger of allowing Dr. Seuss characters to become

*The National Education Association dubbed March 2 The Cat in the Hat Day.*

public domain. Since copyrights expire in seventy-five years, some of his concepts and characters were on the threshold of becoming public. Unauthorized Dr. Seuss merchandise was appearing in stores across the country. Some of it portrayed his characters engaged in objectionable behavior. To prevent this, Mrs. Geisel—who had legal rights to all her late husband's copyrights—had Dr. Seuss's creative property trademarked. That way, no one could use the likeness of any Seuss character without her express permission. Although illegal trademark infringements could still occur on a small scale, there would no longer be a mass market of items such as T-shirts sporting a drunken Cat in the Hat.

Once the trademark was in place, companies began to approach Mrs. Geisel about legally obtaining the right to use Dr. Seuss characters. One of the first organiza-

tions she gave permission to was the clothing designer Esprit. For the 1994 holiday season, Esprit developed a line of clothing and apparel called Seuss Wear. It was such an enormous success that they extended their license agreement, and there is now a full line of Dr. Seuss merchandise available year-round, including ties, watches, shirts, and even shoes. These items are marketed in retail outlets all over the country, as well as on the Internet.

## DR. SEUSS ENTERS THE THIRD DIMENSION

Perhaps the biggest battle to obtain the Seuss license was fought by Universal Studios in Orlando, Florida. They were building a new theme park called Islands of Adventure and wanted one of the themed islands to be a kind of Seussland. The company approached Audrey Geisel for permission in the early planning stages, back in 1993, and she flatly refused. Her husband had been a stern perfectionist, never putting his name on anything that didn't meet his impossibly high standards. Audrey scrutinized all the Seuss proposals that came before her with the same critical eye. She was concerned that the park would cheapen the image of Dr. Seuss. However, after Universal official flew her to Florida to see sketches and concepts, Audrey began to listen. The

## FIRST IMPRESSIONS

*In the guidebook that accompanied the San Diego Museum of Art's retrospective on the works of Dr. Seuss, Steven L. Brezzo, the museum's director, commented on the impression Dr. Seuss's stories made on him as a young child.*

"I was, like children everywhere . . . , being introduced to a new and important wonder of the childhood world: an author who neither preached nor conspired against honest-to-gosh childhood whims; a writer-illustrator whose stories addressed the wild and woolly logic of real kids longing to immerse themselves in books that tickled their boundless fancies and lifted their literary spirits. It was as if my schoolmates and I had just made the acquaintance of a new and exciting secret playmate; a buddy who, although not always scrupulously well mannered according to the tenets of the adult world, could be counted on to provide a fantastic refuge of wacky characters, convoluted logic, and silly vocabulary. And miraculously, grown-ups not only stood by while we reveled in the books, they actually condoned the stuff!

Here, at last was 'children's literature' without the timidity and oversentimentality of traditional works yet which conformed to the features of classic picture-book narratives. The stories were replete with action involving wonderfully endearing characters, they contained frequent changes in imaginative and colorful scenery and were sustained by a narrative that led the reader in a comfortably symmetrical literary direction. This, however, was an assessment that I would apply to the works many years later. To me and my childhood lit-mates, first discovering the joys of independent reading, Dr. Seuss immediately became a synonym for lively and fanciful adventures."

designers reworked plans over and over, striving to convince her that the project was going to be produced on a level never before seen in a theme park. Eventually she decided that the project would do justice to the life's work of her late husband and, in 1995, she gave her permission.

Seuss Landing at Universal Studios Florida allows people to walk in to the pages of many of their most beloved childhood stories. Audrey Geisel retained a lot of creative control during its construction, and it shows. No expense was spared, and there is hardly a single straight line on the island.

To re-create true Seussian architecture, including a never-ending, upside-down staircase, the building facades were all carved—at seemingly impossible angles—out of foam. In addition, more than five hundred different colors of paint were used to decorate the area. Designers even went to southern Florida to harvest live palm trees that grow at strange angles as a result of a powerful hurricane years earlier.

Seuss Landing has rides, shows, costumed characters, walk-through exhibits, food, and the largest selection of Dr. Seuss merchandise found in any one place on earth. There is an interactive play area for small children based on *If I Ran the Zoo* and even a snack stand designed to look like an enormous helping of green eggs and ham (as might be expected, the food available at this location is a green eggs and ham sandwich). There is also a re-creation of the Once-ler's tower in the midst of a devastated Truffula forest with a plaque at the end that contains the Lorax's final words: "Unless someone like you cares a whole awful lot, nothing is going to get better, it's not."[105] The Caro-Seussel contains fifty-four different mounts, each one representing a bizarre Dr. Seuss character. There is a *One Fish Two Fish Red Fish Blue Fish* ride, and guests can even eat under the big top in a cafeteria styled after *If I Ran the Circus*.

*The Caro-Seuss-el at Seuss Landing in Universal Studios in Florida gives celebrities Courtney Cox and David Arquette a momentary escape from adult life.*

*Young children gather on March 2, 2000 in Leland, Mississippi to celebrate the late Dr. Seuss's birthday.*

The heart of Seuss Landing, however, is the Cat in the Hat ride. The structure stands out in the center of the island and is topped by a giant red and white striped hat that rises several stories above the roof. Once inside, guests sit on a couch that takes them through a re-creation of *The Cat in the Hat* tale. More than 130 special effects and thirty animatronic characters help tell the story. Some of the bizarre effects are specifically designed to help the rider capture the nonsensical lack of reality that exists in the book itself, including a revolving, perception-altering twenty-four-foot tunnel. The entire island is an amazing homage to the creative spirit that ran through Dr. Seuss.

## THE IMMORTAL DR. SEUSS

In his youth, Theodor Geisel's aspiration was to write the great American novel and perhaps teach English literature. As he followed his dreams, expressed himself with unerring conviction, and allowed himself to experience all that life had to offer, he accomplished much more than that. His children's books evolved from a string of fun and fanciful successes into an American institution. Today, the name Dr. Seuss is synonymous with both laughter and learning. Although he has been gone for many years, his works continue to delight and inspire children of all ages around the globe. The legacy of Dr. Seuss seems destined to live on forever.

# Notes

## Introduction: "An Imagination with a Long Tail"

1. Quoted in E. J. Kahn Jr., "Children's Friend," *New Yorker*, December 17, 1960, p. 47.

2. Quoted in D. Freeman, "Who Thunk You Up, Dr. Seuss?" *San Jose Mercury News*, June 15, 1969, p. 12.

3. Helen Renthal, "25 Years of Working Wonder with Words," *Chicago Tribune*, November 11, 1962, Part 4, p. 4.

## Chapter 1: Dr. Seuss's First Childhood

4. Quoted in Freeman, "Who Thunk You Up, Dr. Seuss?" p. 12.

5. Quoted in Judith and Neil Morgan, *Dr. Seuss and Mr. Geisel*. New York: Random House, 1995, p. 11.

6. Quoted in Robert Sullivan, "The Boy Who Drew Wynnmphs," *Yankee Magazine*, December 1995, p. 58.

7. Quoted in P. W. Bernstein, "The Unforgettable Dr. Seuss," *Readers Digest*, April 1992, p. 62.

8. Quoted in Sullivan, "The Boy Who Drew Wynnmphs," p. 120.

9. Quoted in Sullivan, "The Boy Who Drew Wynnmphs," p. 120.

10. Quoted in Herbert Kupferberg, "A Seussian Celebration," *Parade*, February 26, 1984, p. 5.

11. Quoted in Edward Connery Lathem, "The Beginnings of Dr. Seuss: A Conversation with Theodor S. Geisel," in Thomas Fensch, ed., *Of Sneetches and Whos and the Good Dr. Seuss*. Jefferson, NC: McFarland, 1997, p. 64.

## Chapter 2: The Struggling Cartoonist

12. Quoted in Morgan, *Dr. Seuss and Mr. Geisel*, p. 47.

13. Quoted in Morgan, *Dr. Seuss and Mr. Geisel*, p. 47.

14. Quoted in Morgan, *Dr. Seuss and Mr. Geisel*, p. 54.

15. Quoted in Lathem, "The Beginnings of Dr. Seuss," p. 68.

16. Quoted in Morgan, *Dr. Seuss and Mr. Geisel*, p. 62.

17. *Dr. Seuss from Then to Now: A Catalogue of the Retrospective Exhibition*. New York: Random House, 1986, p. 23.

18. Quoted in Lathem, "The Beginnings of Dr. Seuss," p. 70.

19. Quoted in C. G. Dowling, "Dr. Seuss," *Life*, July 1989, p. 106.

20. Quoted in Morgan, *Dr. Seuss and Mr. Geisel*, p. 72.

21. Quoted in Morgan, *Dr. Seuss and Mr. Geisel*, p. 80.

22. Dr. Seuss, *And to Think That I Saw It on Mulberry Street*. New York: Vanguard, 1937.

23. Quoted in Morgan, *Dr. Seuss and Mr. Geisel*, p. 83.

24. Dr. Seuss, *And to Think That I Saw It on Mulberry Street*.

25. Dr. Seuss, *And to Think That I Saw It on Mulberry Street*.

26. Stefan Kanfer, "The Doctor Beloved by All," *Time*, October 7, 1991, p. 71.

## Chapter 3: An Explosive Career Begins

27. Quoted in Kahn, "Children's Friend," p. 93.

28. E. Pace, "Dr. Seuss, Modern Mother Goose, Dies," *New York Times*, September 26, 1991, p. A1.

29. Quoted in Peter Bunzel, "His Mind Has Never Grown Up," *Life*, April 6, 1959, p. 113.

30. Quoted in Cynthia G. La Ferle, "Oh, the Places Dr. Seuss Has Taken Us!" *Christian Science Monitor*, March 2, 1998, p. 11.

31. Dr. Seuss, *If I Ran the Zoo*. New York: Random House, 1950.

32. Dr. Seuss, *If I Ran the Zoo*.

33. Chet Raymo, "Dr. Seuss and Dr. Einstein: Children's Books and Scientific Imagination," in Fensch, *Of Sneetches and Whos and the Good Dr. Seuss*. Jefferson, NC: McFarland, 1997, p. 170.

34. Dr. Seuss, *On Beyond Zebra!* New York: Random House, 1955.

35. Ruth K. MacDonald, *Dr. Seuss*. Boston: Twayne, 1988, p. 165.

36. Dr. Seuss, *Yertle the Turtle and Other Stories*. New York: Random House, 1958.

37. Dr. Seuss, *Yertle the Turtle and Other Stories*.

38. Quoted in Bunzel, "His Mind Has Never Grown Up," p. 113.

39. Quoted in Bunzel, "His Mind Has Never Grown Up," p. 113.

40. Quoted in Bunzel, "His Mind Has Never Grown Up," p. 110.

41. Quoted in Dowling, "Dr. Seuss," p. 106.

42. Quoted in Dowling, "Dr. Seuss," p. 107.

## *Chapter 4: The Cat Who Taught Kids to Read*

43. "Life with the Authors: The Name—Ted Geisel," *Newsweek*, June 6, 1960, p. 115.

44. Mary Lystad, *From Dr. Mather to Dr. Seuss: 200 Years of American Books for Children*. Boston: G. K. Hall, 1980, p. 201.

45. Dr. Seuss, *The Cat in the Hat*. New York: Random House, 1957.

46. Quoted in Judith Frutig, "Dr. Seuss's Green-Eggs-and-Ham World," in Fensch, *Of Sneetches and Whos and the Good Dr. Seuss*. pp. 79–80.

47. Kahn, "Children's Friend," p. 50.

48. Quoted in Elizabeth B. Moje and Woan-Ru Shyu, "The Places You've Taken Us, Dr. Seuss," *Reading Teacher*, May 1992, p. 675.

49. Rita Roth, "On Beyond Zebra with Dr. Seuss," in Fensch, *Of Sneetches and Whos and the Good Dr. Seuss*. Jefferson, NC: McFarland, 1997, p. 143.

50. Clifton Fadiman, *Six by Seuss: A Treasury of Dr. Seuss Classics*. New York: Random House, 1991, p. 7.

51. Quoted in "'Somebody's Got to Win' in Kids' Books: An Interview with Dr. Seuss on His Books for Children, Young and Old," *U.S. News & World Report*, April 14, 1986, p. 69.

52. Quoted in Kahn, "Children's Friend," p. 92.

53. Quoted in Kahn, "Children's Friend," p. 93.

54. Quoted in Warren T. Greenleaf, "How the Grinch Stole Reading: The Serious Nonsense of Dr. Seuss," in Fensch, *Of Sneetches and Whos and the Good Dr. Seuss*, Jefferson, NC: McFarland, 1997, p. 143.

55. Quoted in Kahn, "Children's Friend," p. 92.

56. Quoted in Glenn Edward Sadler, "Maurice Sendak and Dr. Seuss: A Conversation," in Fensch, *Of Sneetches and Whos and the Good Dr. Seuss*, Jefferson, NC: McFarland, 1997, p. 139.

57. Quoted in Jonathan Cott,"The Good Dr. Seuss,"in Fensch, *Of Sneetches and Whos and the Good Dr. Seuss*, Jefferson, NC: McFarland, 1997, p. 114.

58. Quoted in Hilliard Harper, "The Private World of Dr. Seuss: A Visit to Theodor Geisel's La Jolla Mountaintop," in Fensch, *Of Sneetches and Whos and the Good Dr. Seuss*, Jefferson, NC: McFarland, 1997, p. 132.

59. Quoted in Don Freeman, "Dr. Seuss at 72—Going Like 60," *Saturday Evening Post*, March 1977, p. 8.

60. Quoted in Cynthia Gorney, "Dr. Seuss at 75: Grinch, Cat in Hat, Wocket and Generations of Kids in His Pocket," *Washington Post*, May 21, 1979, pp. B1, B3.

61. Quoted in Bunzel, "His Mind Has Never Grown Up," p. 113.

### Chapter 5: From Politics to Animation

62. Quoted in Morgan, *Dr. Seuss and Mr. Geisel*, p. 101.

63. Quoted in Richard H. Minear, *Dr. Seuss Goes to War*. New York: New Press, 1999, p. 45.

64. Quoted in Morgan, *Dr. Seuss and Mr. Geisel*, p. 104.

65. Quoted in Morgan, *Dr. Seuss and Mr. Geisel*, p. 147.

66. Quoted in Dowling, "Dr. Seuss," p. 106.

67. Quoted in Morgan, *Dr. Seuss and Mr. Geisel*, p. 135.

68. Quoted in MacDonald, *Dr. Seuss*, p. 104.

69. Fadiman, *Six by Seuss*, p. 8.

70. Dr. Seuss, *How the Grinch Stole Christmas!* New York: Random House, 1957.

### Chapter 6: The Message Books

71. Quoted in Bunzel, "His Mind Has Never Grown Up," p. 113.

72. Dr. Seuss, *Horton Hatches the Egg*. New York: Random House, 1940.

73. Quoted in Kahn, "Children's Friend," p. 67.

74. Dr. Seuss, *Horton Hears a Who!* New York: Random House, 1954.

75. "'Somebody's Got to Win' in Kids' Books," *U.S. News & World Report*, p. 69.

76. Quoted in Cott, "The Good Dr. Seuss," p. 118.

77. Quoted in Cott, "The Good Dr. Seuss," p. 118.

78. Dr. Seuss, *The Sneetches and Other Stories*. New York: Random House, 1961.

79. Quoted in Cott, "The Good Dr. Seuss," p. 118.

80. "'Somebody's Got to Win' in Kids' Books," *U.S. News & World Report*, p. 69.

81. Dr. Seuss, *The Lorax*. New York: Random House, 1971.

82. Jennifer Zicht, "In Pursuit of the Lorax," *EPA Journal*, September/October 1991, p. 27.

83. Quoted in Ron Arias, "A Boy Sides with Dr. Seuss's Lorax, and Puts a Town at Loggerheads," *People*, October 23, 1989, pp. 67–68.

84. Quoted in Ron Arias, "A Boy Sides with Dr. Seuss's Lorax, and Puts a Town at Loggerheads," p. 68.

85. Quoted in Gorney, "Dr. Seuss at 75," p. 88.

86. Quoted in Pace, "Dr. Seuss, Modern Mother Goose, Dies," p. D23.

87. Dr. Seuss, *You're Only Old Once!* New York: Random House, 1986.

88. "'Somebody's Got to Win' in Kids' Books," *U.S. News & World Report*, p. 69.

89. Quoted in Dowling, "Dr. Seuss," p. 105.

### Chapter 7: The Immortal Dr. Seuss

90. Quoted in Lathem, "The Beginnings of Dr. Seuss," p. 75.

91. Quoted in Morgan, *Dr. Seuss and Mr. Geisel*, p. 234.

92. Dr. Seuss, *Green Eggs and Ham!* New York: Random House, 1960.

93. Quoted in Morgan, *Dr. Seuss and Mr. Geisel*, p. 255.

94. Quoted in Morgan, *Dr. Seuss and Mr. Geisel*, p. 266.

95. Quoted in Morgan, *Dr. Seuss and Mr. Geisel*, p. 289.

96. Pace, "Dr. Seuss, Modern Mother Goose, Dies," p. A1.

97. Quoted in Cott, "The Good Dr. Seuss," p. 117.

98. Quoted in Morgan, *Dr. Seuss and Mr. Geisel*, p. 290.

99. Kanfer, "The Doctor Beloved by All," p. 71.

100. Quoted in Cott, "The Good Dr. Seuss," p. 118.

101. Quoted in Calmetta Y. Coleman, "First the Grinch Stole Christmas, Now He's Hard at Work Selling It," *Wall Street Journal*, December 24, 1998, p. B1.

102. Quoted in Tim Cornell, "Honoring Seuss, the Man Who Put a Hat on the Cat," *Christian Science Monitor*, November 20, 1997, p. 22.

103. Barbara Kantrowitz and Anne Underwood, "Dyslexia and the New Science of Reading," *Newsweek*, November 22, 1999, p. 77.

104. Quoted in Tim Cornell, "The Cat in the Hat Throws a Party to Get Kids to Read," *Christian Science Monitor*, February 25, 1998, p. 15.

105. Dr. Seuss, *The Lorax*.

# For Further Reading

## Books

Dr. Seuss, *The Lorax*. New York: Random House, 1971. An environmental tale that warns of the dangers of despoiling the environment. Complete with the typical Seuss drawings and rhyme, this book is both fun and meaningful.

————, *Oh, the Places You'll Go!* New York: Random House, 1989. Dr. Seuss's final book is the story of a child who ventures out into the world to see what is in store for him. It is an inspirational story that focuses on hope and following your dreams.

————, *You're Only Old Once!* New York: Random House, 1986. Born of the frustration Dr. Seuss felt at the way the medical industry treated the elderly, this book tells the story of an anonymous gentleman trying to keep a stiff upper lip in the face of ailing health, grueling medical tests, and unsympathetic doctors.

*Dr. Seuss from Then to Now: A Catalogue of the Retrospective Exhibition*. New York: Random House, 1986. Originally created as a companion to Dr. Seuss's museum exhibition, which premiered at the San Diego Museum of Art, this book contains a brief biography as well as a complete list of every item displayed at the event. It also contains a number of rare and unusual illustrations.

Ruth K. MacDonald, *Dr. Seuss*. Boston: Twayne, 1988. An easy-to-read yet comprehensive book on the life and works of Theodor Seuss Geisel. It includes basic biographical information as well as an overview and analysis of most of his more well known works.

Judith and Neil Morgan, *Dr. Seuss and Mr. Geisel*. New York: Random House, 1995. Written by a couple who were good friends with Geisel, this full-length biography contains many personal stories about his life that are unavailable in any other sources. It is a chronological overview of every aspect of Ted's life, from his parents' lineage, through his personal and professional struggles, to his final days.

Maryann N. Weidt, *Oh, the Places He Went: A Story About Dr. Seuss*. Minneapolis, MN: Carolrhoda Books, 1994. A biography written in narrative form for the very young reader.

## Periodicals

"Island Is Nothing Less than Seussian," *Amusement Business*, April 5, 1999. Describes the new attraction at Universal Studios Orlando that has been designed as a three-dimensional, interactive version of Dr. Seuss's books.

Ron Arias, "A Boy Sides with Dr. Seuss's Lorax, and Puts a Town at Loggerheads," *People*, October 23, 1989. A very interesting article about a town divided over issues of whether logging is an acceptable local industry. At the center of the controversy is the question of whether or not to take *The Lorax* off the local school shelves.

Cynthia Gorney, "Dr. Seuss at 75: Grinch, Cat in Hat, Wocket and Generations of Kids in His Pocket," *Washington Post*, May 21, 1979. A great retrospective article about Dr. Seuss's career, in honor of his seventy-fifth birthday.

Sue Monk Kidd, "Turning Loose," *Guideposts*, September 1991. This article is a touching story of how a mother used Dr. Seuss to help ease the pain of watching her son leave home for college.

Alison Lurie, "The Cabinet of Dr. Seuss," *New York Review of Books*, December 20, 1990. Discusses how Dr. Seuss's books progressed from his early days to his later "message" books.

# Works Consulted

## Books

Clifton Fadiman, *Six by Seuss: A Treasury of Dr. Seuss Classics*. New York: Random House, 1991. An in-depth look at why Dr. Seuss's books are so good at helping young children learn to read.

Thomas Fensch, ed., *Of Sneetches and Whos and the Good Dr. Seuss*. Jefferson, NC: McFarland, 1997. A valuable collection of some of the best articles written on Theodor Geisel over the course of his lengthy career and life.

Mary Lystad, *From Dr. Mather to Dr. Seuss: 200 Years of American Books for Children*. Boston: G. K. Hall, 1980. Discusses Dr. Seuss's place in the history of children's literature.

Selma G. Lanes, *Down the Rabbit Hole*. New York: Atheneum, 1971. This book is a critical analysis of children's picture books from the 1940s through the 1980s. It explores the rapid increase in publishing and popularity of such books, as well as what true literary merit they may have.

Richard H. Minear, *Dr. Seuss Goes to War*. New York: New Press, 1999. Published in 1999 amidst a resurgence in Dr. Seuss's popularity, this book is a collection of his early political cartoons. These works represent a time in Dr. Seuss's life when his hard-edged humor was allowed to surface, nearly unfiltered.

Dr. Seuss, *And to Think That I Saw it on Mulberry Street*. New York: Vanguard, 1937. Dr. Seuss's first book, it tells the story of a young boy's boredom with the ordinary sights to be seen in his hometown and his subsequent creation of a grand, imaginary parade.

———, *Green Eggs and Ham!* New York: Random House, 1960. Written on a bet, this book targeted an even younger audience than Seuss's prior Beginner Books. It met with more success than anyone had anticipated and went on to become his best-selling work.

———, *Horton Hatches the Egg*. New York: Random House, 1940. Seuss's last book before joining World War II, this is the story of a noble elephant who, despite foul weather, attempts on his life, and being abducted into a traveling circus, maintains his pledge to watch over a bird's egg.

———, *Horton Hears a Who!* New York: Random House, 1954. With the return of Horton, Dr. Seuss creates a tale of minority rights, centered around a tiny community of creatures in danger of being destroyed by the cruelty and ignorance of a mob of forest animals.

———, *How the Grinch Stole Christmas!* New York: Random House, 1957. The classic tale of an angry creature who sought to steal the entire holiday of

Christmas from the small town of Whoville.

———, *If I Ran the Zoo*. New York: Random House, 1950. A young boy by the name of Gerald McGrew imagines the fantastic creatures he would find for the local zoo if he were in charge.

———, *On Beyond Zebra!* New York: Random House, 1955. One of Dr. Seuss's strongest arguments against the limitations of the human capacity to learn and imagine, it tells the story of all the amazing letters, and the wonderous things they represent, which come after the letter Z.

———, *The Cat in the Hat*. New York: Random House, 1957. With his stovepipe hat, charm, and knack for chaos, the cat in the hat has become one of the most recognizable figures in children's literature. Originally designed as a replacement for the boring reading primers of its era, this book has been used throughout the decades both to entertain and to introduce the concept of reading to young children.

———, *The Sneetches and Other Stories*. New York: Random House, 1961. Another collection of short stories featuring stories about stubbornness, a scary pair of pants, and some birdlike creatures who learn the senselessness of prejudice.

———, *Yertle the Turtle and Other Stories*. New York: Random House, 1958. A collection of stories including a tale about a fascist turtle who was obsessed with being king over all he could see.

**Periodicals**

P. W. Bernstein, "The Unforgettable Dr. Seuss," *Readers Digest*, April 1992. A warm remembrance of the impact Dr. Seuss had on one person who worked with him at Random House.

Peter Bunzel, "His Mind Has Never Grown Up," *Life*, April 6, 1959. A short but interesting account of Dr. Seuss's life and work.

Nancy Carlsson-Paige and Diane E. Levin, "*The Butter Battle Book: Uses and Abuses with Young Children*," *Young Children*, 1986. A review of *The Butter Battle Book* that discusses the impact the book can have on young children.

Calmetta Y. Coleman, "First the Grinch Stole Christmas, Now He's Hard at Work Selling It," *Wall Street Journal*, December 24, 1998. A critical look at how Dr. Seuss's Grinch character is being used to sell Christmas products despite the antimaterialism message of the book.

Tim Cornell, "The Cat in the Hat Throws a Party to Get Kids to Read," *Christian Science Monitor*, February 25, 1998. Discusses the conceptualization and implementation of the first Read Across America Day in honor of Ted Geisel's birthday.

———, "Honoring Seuss, the Man Who Put a Hat on the Cat," *Christian Science Monitor*, November 20, 1997. Discusses the memorial statue garden that is being built in Geisel's hometown of Springfield, Massachusetts.

C. G. Dowling, "Dr. Seuss," *Life*, July 1989. A short account of the life and works of Dr. Seuss.

Dr. Seuss, "But for Grown Ups, Laughing Isn't Any Fun," *New York Times Book Review*, November 16, 1952. This unusual article written by Dr. Seuss discusses his philosophy about the part of children's sense of humor that dies when they grow up.

D. Freeman, *San Jose Mercury News*, June 15, 1969. An article which discusses Dr. Seuss's increasing popularity and attempts to uncover some secrets about his writing style.

Don Freeman, "Dr. Seuss at 72—Going Like 60," *Saturday Evening Post*, March 1977. This article discusses Dr. Seuss's unwavering string of both critically and commercially successful books.

John Garvey, "Guns and Butter: Dr. Seuss's Liberal Sentimentality," *Commonweal*, August 10, 1984. A primarily negative review of Dr. Seuss's *The Butter Battle Book* that condemns the book for oversimplifying the issue of warfare.

Greg Gatusso, "Cereal Maker Fights Illiteracy," *Fund Raising Management*, March 1993. A brief report on the collaboration between Kellogg Cereal Company and the Dr. Seuss Foundation to help bring books to the needy.

Catherine Hinman, "Universal Proud of Diverse Characters," *Orlando Sentinel*, April 18, 1999. Highlights a new theme park scheduled to open in central Florida, including an island dedicated to Dr. Seuss.

Ann Hulbert, "They Won't Grow Up," *New York Times Book Review*, November 12, 1995. This short article discusses the childlike quality of four influential authors of children's literature.

"Speaking for the Truffula Trees," *International Wildlife*, May/June 1999. A one page excerpt from *The Lorax*.

E. J. Kahn Jr., "Children's Friend," *New Yorker*, December 17, 1960. One of the first in-depth biographies written on the life of Theodor Geisel. Covering everything from his early childhood to his life in the hills of San Diego, this article is perhaps the most useful early resource for information on the man behind Dr. Seuss.

Stefan Kanfer, "The Doctor Beloved by All," *Time*, October 7, 1991. An article that appeared one week after Geisel had died. Honoring his life, it celebrated his many achievements.

Barbara Kantrowitz and Anne Underwood, "Dyslexia and the New Science of Reading," *Newsweek*, November 22, 1999. This article discusses some of the most recent advances in the understanding of dyslexia. It focuses on how the disease affects the normal functioning of the human brain.

Herbert Kupferberg, "A Seussian Celebration," *Parade*, February 26, 1984. An early look at the life and times of Dr. Seuss.

———, "Dr. Seuss Heads for Home," *Palm Beach Post Parade*, June 7, 1998. Discusses the Springfield Memorial being constructed to honor Dr. Seuss, its most famous resident.

Cynthia G. La Ferle, "Oh, the Places Dr. Seuss Has Taken Us!" *Christian Science Monitor*, March 2, 1998. An article that remembers the late Dr. Seuss on his birthday and discusses Read Across America Day.

Joshua LeBeau, "Freud on Seuss," *Koala Newspaper*, 1989. An amusing review of *The Cat in the Hat* as interpreted by a student of Sigmund Freud.

Elizabeth B. Moje and Woan-Ru Shyu, "The Places You've Taken Us, Dr. Seuss," *Reading Teacher*, May 1992. An essay written by teachers about the impact Dr. Seuss had on them.

*Newsweek*, "Life with the Authors: The Name—Ted Geisel," June 6, 1960. A quick biographical account of the life of Ted Geisel.

E. Pace, "Dr. Seuss, Modern Mother Goose, Dies," *New York Times*, September 26, 1991. An obituary article that appeared the day after he died.

Helen Renthal, "25 Years of Working Wonder with Words," *Chicago Tribune*, November 11, 1962. Discusses the reasons why people are fascinated with Dr. Seuss's works.

Robert Sullivan, "The Boy Who Drew Wynnmphs," *Yankee Magazine*, December 1995. A light account of Dr. Seuss's early influences.

"'Somebody's Got to Win' in Kids' Books: An Interview with Dr. Seuss on His Books for Children, Young and Old," *U.S. News & World Report*, April 14, 1986. A very short interview with Dr. Seuss after the publication of *You're Only Old Once!*

Bob Warren, "Dr. Seuss, Former *Jacko* Editor, Tells How Boredom May Lead to Success," *Dartmouth*, May 10, 1934. One of the very first interviews ever given by Ted Geisel. This article was written before he wrote his first children's book and focuses on his successful advertising career.

Jennifer Zicht, "In Pursuit of the Lorax," *EPA Journal*, September/October 1991. A lengthy article about the importance of starting conservation education at an early age, it begins with a glowing review of *The Lorax* as a perfect example of what children should be reading.

# Index

# Picture Credits

Cover photo: Corbis/Bettmann
AP/Delta Democrat Times, 97
AP/Journal Gazette, 38
AP/NYPD, 70
AP/The Day, 56
AP/The Morning Journal, 48
AP/The New Press, 61, 88
AP/Universal Studios, 96
AP/Wide World Photos, 13, 32, 35, 36, 39, 52, 69, 71, 79, 86, 94
Archive Photos/Gene Lester, 12, 42, 50
Corbis, 18, 83

Corbis/James L. Amos, 58
Corbis/Bettmann, 27, 29, 65, 81
Corbis/Rick Doyle, 75
Corbis/Mitchell Gerber, 91
Corbis/E. O. Hoppe, 24
Corbis/Hulton-Deutsch, 66
Corbis/Phil Schermeister, 77
Corbis/Yogi, Inc., 21
Culver Pictures, Inc., 23, 62
Library of Congress, 44
National Archives, 15

# About the Author

Stuart P. Levine currently works as a wildlife educator in central Florida. Having degrees in both psychology and wildlife education has allowed him to work in such diverse fields as psychiatric counseling, zookeeping, and writing. His other published works for Lucent are in the Endangered Animals and Habitat series, including *The Elephant*, *The Tiger*, and *The Orangutan*.